Open Hands:
Lessons on Giving and Receiving

BRIGHT SKY PRESS

2365 Rice Blvd., Suite 202 Houston, Texas 77005
Box 416, Albany, Texas 76430

10   9   8   7   6   5   4   3   2   1

Library of Congress Cataloging-in Publication Data

Mullins, Jana, 1953-
Open hands : lessons on giving and receiving / by Jana Mullins.
p. cm.
ISBN 978-1-933979-33-5 (hardcover : alk. paper) 1. Generosity—Religious aspects—
Christianity. 2. Gratitude—Religious aspects—Christianity. I. Title.

BV4647.G45M85 2008
241'.677—dc22

2008015932

Book and cover design by Ellen Peeples Cregan
Printed in China through Asia Pacific Offset

Open Hands:
Lessons on Giving and Receiving

Jana Mullins

JANA MULLINS

BRIGHT SKY PRESS
HOUSTON, TEXAS – ALBANY, TEXAS

To my children,
Jessica, Andrew and Leslie,
who give me immeasurable joy in every way.
You are the most precious gifts
I have ever received.

"To receive everything,
one must open one's hands and give"

TAISEN DESHIMARU

CONTENTS

"Each day offers us the gift of being a special occasion if we can simply learn that as well as giving, it is blessed to receive with grace and a grateful heart."

SARAH BREATHWACH

"You give but little when you
give of your possessions.
It is when you give of yourself
that you truly give."

KAHLIL GIBRAN, THE PROPHET

Acknowledgments

Abundant blessings and amazing moments of giving and receiving have touched and changed my life as a result of this book. I am humbled and deeply grateful to every individual who submitted a story. While I was unable to include all of them, every entry touched me deeply. Your giving and receiving hearts are interwoven on every page of this book.

Thank you dear colleagues and friends. You all took this journey with me. (I include even my dog, Hercules the Great, who kept me company on many sleepless nights.) Without you this book, this collection of stories, would have been impossible. To Nancy Burdess and Sam Sheff, two very special friends who encouraged and supported me from the first moment I spoke of this book as a possibility: thank you from the bottom of my heart! You held this vision with me, even during moments when it was hard for me to see it myself!

To Ellen Peeples Cregan, whose striking graphics and generous spirit brought life to this book; to Michael Hart who introduced me to Ellen and contributed many beautiful photographs featured within these pages; to Steve Barnhill, my neighbor and friend, whose encouragement, editing, and sage advice, kept me brief, honest, and on schedule: thank you!

To Terry Bell, President of Rockwell Fund, Inc. and Rockwell's trustees: thank you for the time and patience you gave me these past two years to pursue my graduate degree. Your support has been genuinely appreciated.

To Jill Pickett, my mentor and friend, who for eight years has celebrated and shared in my life's transitions and growing pains: thank you!

To Judy Ahlgrim, Domingo Barrios, Peggy Boice, Susie Dalebout, Steve Davidson, Angela Caughlin, Debbie Cavanaugh, Elena Cave, Karen Clifton, Debbie Dalton, Nancy Frees Fountain, Barbara Henley, Lynn Hoster, Murray Kast, Russanne Kelley, Shoshana Levine, Chris Lukens, Linda May, Jim McLean, Quynh-Anh McMahan, Gail McWilliams, Rita Mills, Teryl Morrow, Tom Nall, Lidya Osadchey, Esther Perrine, Charles Rhodes, Mollie Romanek, Sara Selber, Suzi Slater, Richard Torres, Kerri Washburn, Carolyn Watson, Christine Weissman (oh, that amazing website design!) and Mary Zierke: thank you all for listening, reading, writing, typing and providing "You can do it! You're almost there!" encouragement. Each one of you in your own extraordinary way, helped to bolster me through this time, and I am grateful.

To Ron Hulnick, President, and Mary Hulnick, Chief Academic Officer of the University of Santa Monica; to Lili Goodman, my faculty advisor; to my project team members Jim Bagnola, Janice Dempsey, Suzie Gueldner, and my classmates at the University: thank you for your life-changing learning, heart-centered listening, and a joyous and challenging two years. I take with me an incredible wealth of knowledge, a new way of living and being, and memories for a lifetime. I am forever grateful!

To my remarkable parents, Mary and Bernard Mullins, my sisters Monica and Sheila, and my brother Matt: thank you for your unending love throughout my life. Words cannot express the deep love I hold in my heart for you. How enormously blessed I feel every day to be a part of our family.

And to our God, the perfect Giver and Receiver, who loves each one of us unconditionally just as we are: I praise and thank You with open hands for all You have given me, and I hope I have been, and always will be, a gracious receiver.

Jana

Introduction

It started with a visit to the University of Santa Monica admissions office. As a single mother with three children, I had a dream of pursuing graduate studies. However, at this time in my life, that would have been nearly impossible—had it not been for my friend, Fred.

Fred believed in me more than I believed in myself. He said, "Apply for the scholarship, Jana, and if you get it, I will pay your monthly round trip air fare from Houston to California."

In my mind, the odds of getting the scholarship were slim to none. There would be so many people applying. I knew I didn't have a chance. And even if I did, how could I possibly accept this generous gift from my friend?

It wasn't until two weeks after Fred's offer I decided to swallow my pride, take the risk of not being accepted and apply.

Months later I received a call from the university telling me I was not only accepted into the graduate program but I would receive the scholarship. I couldn't believe it! My dream of pursuing a graduate degree was coming true; however, graciously receiving my friend's offer was harder than I ever realized.

I later accepted Fred's gift and, every month before my class weekend, my email ticket would arrive and, every time I boarded my plane, tears would well up in my eyes.

My friend provided much more than the gift of airfare to school. He provided the encouragement I needed at a time in my life when I was feeling "not quite good enough" inside. His generous giving, which taught me the life-changing lesson of being a gracious receiver, was also the inspiration for this book.

Bringing together this remarkable collection of stories about giving and receiving has been inspiring, too. The thought of how to undertake such an endeavor was way beyond my wildest imagination, stretching me far more than I anticipated. As I began to share my vision for this book, which would require me to take that trembling first step and "ask" for stories and assistance, I began to experience the incredible support and generosity of individuals willing to give and soon came to realize that this book was not just about giving, but also about the transforming power in learning to accept and to graciously receive. As I opened my heart and became present to those sometimes "too tiny to notice" moments God gives us every day—a hug from a child, a kind word from a coworker, a good morning call from a friend—I became aware that the "circle of giving" remains incomplete unless a gift is both given and received with an open heart and open hands.

As you read the stories in this book you will see every story speaks of a giving with a whisper from God saying "receive." We never know what life has in store. What we do know is that every day God gives each one of us an opportunity to touch a life. Every one of us has something to give. I hope this book inspires you to seize not only the giving moments we have in our lives, but also relish the golden receiving moments that occur every day.

And thanks again, Fred.

A Gift of Green

Ann Thomas Hamilton

While the world focused on the tragic events of September 11, 2001, I endured my own personal "9/11," just eight days after the planes hit the twin towers, the Pentagon and the field in Pennsylvania. On September 19, 2001, I received a call from my primary physician's nurse with news that every woman dreads. I had breast cancer.

The diagnosis suggested that it was a stage one, likely hormone-induced, malignancy which would require a lumpectomy followed by a few radiation treatments. After finding the right surgeon, I entered into the surgery with a positive attitude having been told that it had been caught early, the lump was very small and therefore the prognosis looked good. There was a lingering concern that, because the lump was on the far left side of my left breast, the cancer cells might have spread into my lymph glands. As my very supportive sister, Evelyn said at the time: You don't have breast cancer, you have armpit cancer! Humor has always been a real source of comfort in our family.

The surgery went well, but the lingering concern became reality. The cells had spread into the lymph glands which meant more aggressive treatment: chemotherapy for six months, followed by another surgery to ensure "clean margins" around the surgical site, followed by five weeks of radiation, followed by five years of preventive medication. Wow! So much to absorb! All my cancer-survivor friends advised me to take a year of my life and focus on getting well. Good advice.

This is the backdrop for my story of acceptance and generosity.

In February, 2000, I moved into my wonderful little bungalow in Section One of Garden Oaks, just north of Houston Heights. It had been remodeled by another resident of the neighborhood who has since passed away. John did an incredible job of transforming what had been a very small, degraded, unoccupied house into a warm, cozy, colorful place that I could finally call home, having rented since my arrival in Houston in 1985. The large yard was standard St. Augustine grass, some old unpruned trees, and a few new shrubs planted around the house's perimeter. The Asakuras, my new

14

neighbors to the east, were a family of four: a landscape architect, his wife and their two young daughters. We became fast friends. I greatly admired their beautiful yard and told Keiji, the architect, that I wanted my yard to meld into theirs and create a greater green space to attract more birds, butterflies and wildlife.

Over the next several months, Keiji and I put together a conceptual plan, added topsoil, visited a local organic nursery, and planted a few low-maintenance native plants. Occasionally, he would bring left-over plants from his various client sites and either leave them for me to plant or just do it himself. I kept asking to pay him, but never received a bill. Slowly, my yard began "melding" with the Asakuras' as intended, but it was a "work in progress" when cancer struck.

After my surgery and hospitalization, I spent ten days of recovery with my sister and brother-in-law in their home across town. Having boarded my dogs, the house remained empty save for my housekeepers who picked up the mail and fed the cats daily. The day finally arrived for me to go home for a visit and begin getting my life back. Evelyn drove me and I felt such joy being back in the neighborhood with its lovely little homes, large lawns, big old trees, cool green spaces, and narrow streets. When we pulled into my driveway, we were astounded at the change that had taken place during my absence. The front yard had been transformed from a "work in progress" to a beautiful serpentine garden of wonder—full of a rainbow of diverse grasses, flowering ground cover, and shrubs of every shape and variety. We were speechless! I broke into tears knowing that my gentle, generous neighbor

had undertaken this task of love and kindness as his gift to a worried, sick neighbor. What a gift.

One of the most important lessons I learned during that year of treatment and recovery was to accept the kindness of others and, when needing something, not to be shy in asking for help. Keiji's gift was the start of this personal change from being a fiercely independent woman to one who could seek and accept help from others. After five years, my garden continues to thrive and bloom with fragrance and color. Birds and butterflies abound. Unfortunately, Keiji is no longer my neighbor, but his essence and life force remain in the garden he gave me. I think of him everyday as I walk past this garden so full of life and love, grace and gratitude. It continually nurtures my soul and brings me joy and peace. Thank you, dear Keiji, for this gift of green.

WHEN WE PULLED INTO MY DRIVEWAY, WE WERE ASTOUNDED AT THE CHANGE THAT HAD TAKEN PLACE. THE FRONT YARD HAD BEEN TRANSFORMED FROM A "WORK IN PROGRESS" TO A BEAUTIFUL SERPENTINE GARDEN OF WONDER.

A Quality Point

Murray Kast

It was 1969. A small Jesuit college in the Midwest. The milieu was Woodstock, war and work. It was the year of my graduation; the ostensible starting point into mainstream America, the ending point for college deferments from Vietnam's black hole.

My upbringing, borne of parents scarred from the "great depression," had instilled an aversion to debt that nearly bordered on the irrational. My father, while never having attended a day of high school, earned too much for me to qualify for student aid and too little (raising five children) to divert such financial resources to the benefit of one. My mother—traditional early twentieth century—was devoted but not doting. They were adamant about college, and not just any college. After the completion of twelve years of Catholic primary and secondary education, this was no time to go secular. Notwithstanding that the local Jesuit college, Rockhurst, was four or five times the annual expense of any of several other nearby colleges and notwithstanding that this same Jesuit college's student body was open to males only, this was the college that I would surely prefer to attend.

Not! My parents did suggest that I could get student loans, that such debt was acceptable. My lessons on debt were too well ingrained. With my parents' insistent wishes, I would attend Rockhurst but against their better judgment, I would work full time to pay for it. While eliminating any long term liability, such rigors precluded conferral of my Bachelor's Degree on graduation day in the late spring of the year. It wasn't a dearth of required hours or a missed course in my declared major, I was lacking five "quality points" necessary for successful degree completion. The short version on quality points is that in order to graduate, a student must have at least a "C" average in all courses. Thus for every "D," one must have a "B" somewhere in the mix to compensate, or one "A" would cover two "Ds", an "F" must be offset by an "A," etc., one of those esoteric formulas that have less meaning the further one is distanced. A shortage of quality points was a clear indication that overall class performance was sub par.

My selection for classes was not determined by a specific interest or a favored professor or supposed ease of a course.

16

Nothing so frivolous. No, as I chose my curriculum for each semester, there was but one overriding principle to prepare myself for the business world ahead: all classes must start and be completed between the hours of 8 A.M. and 12 P.M. This, to accommodate a 40-hour or more work-week schedule starting at 1 P.M. and finishing at 9 P.M. So, if Theory of Statistical Analysis—9:00 A.M.—M-W-F was the only "open" class at that hour, that was the choice. In fairness, I did have Tuesdays off from work.

From the second semester until the four years had run their course, I led the scholastic probation list. That meant a twice annual visit to the office of the Academic Dean, Father Weiss SJ, to explain the disappointing (lack of) progress of the previous semester and what remedial action would reverse the situation heading into the next. Each ended with a stern warning that this would be the last extension of such tolerance. Those meetings always took place right after my visit to the Registrar's office to pay for the succeeding semester. A fait accompli. Tuition and erudition are first cousins, if not more closely related. In reality, the primary advantage favorable to allowing me to continue my unabated drift was the absolute certainty that dropping me from school would have meant an immediate review of my "draft" status. In other words, I would have lost my college deferral and would have been on my way to Vietnam within months. A "Catch 22" for a Catholic college.

As my final and most successful academic semester came to a close, it was not enough to overcome the aforementioned five missing quality points, the gulf that separated me from my peers. Since I would not actually receive my diploma, I decided against attending the graduation ceremonies. There

was a young priest, Father Costello SJ, who had been my guidance counselor over the years. He pleaded with me to go through the motions of the graduation for the sake of my family and myself. (At some future date I would realize the significance of it all.) To this day my mother reminds me of the words spoken prior to the final group—my group—as we entered the stage, "The following students will have degrees conferred at a later date.... Unexplainably (Why is this unexplainable? I'd say, "quite explainable") we did not receive the same applause as the first group—the summa cum laude(s).

Summer was just ahead and everyone was talking about finally taking some time off after four tedious years of books, reports and homework. My student deferment was good for a few more months. I decided that maybe I should take a couple of summer school classes to try to make up those quality points; get this all behind me. The bright side of summer school was that it was about seven weeks long; the dark side was that it was every day for two hours, for each class—four concentrated hours every day of the week. So the plan was to take two classes, get an "A" in one and a "B" in the other. I would have exactly the five quality points necessary. Available classes were limited and must still fit into my work schedule.

Like it or not, it was Introduction to Teaching with Mr. Chenot, and "History of the Industrial Revolution with Father Imbs SJ. I had never attended classes from either and so really didn't know them. I kind of "got into" the class on teaching, even thought it might be good for the "A" part of the plan. The Industrial Revolution class was mind numbing—and I needed a "B" here. As the weeks wore on I found myself actually enjoying the teaching class, the history class

17

was like sitting in hell. I'm sure I never scored higher than a "C" (mostly "Ds") on any of the history tests, including the final. As the summer session approached the end I realized my plan, like nearly all of my college time, would fall far short of the initial anticipation.

TWO SIGNIFICANT EVENTS WERE YET TO UNFOLD. A FEW WEEKS LATER I RECEIVED MY DIPLOMA, A BACHELOR OF ARTS DEGREE. A FEW MONTHS LATER I RECEIVED MY MILITARY ORDERS FOR VIETNAM.

At the last teaching class, Mr. Chenot announced that each student would himself determine the appropriate grade for his work in that class. It would be on the honor system. So I could pick my grade. I'm not sure I ever received even one "A" in all my four years. I couldn't bring myself to award one at this point. I turned in my final grade as a "B," what I thought I was deserving. From the history class the very best I could hope for was a "C" but was more likely to be a "D," adding yet another quality point to the existing deficit. The fault lay clearly on my shoulders. It meant that at some future date I would have to return to take yet more classes to pick up three or four or more quality points. The time, the expense, the frustration.

Early the next morning I received a call from Mr. Chenot. He asked if I had time to come in to talk with him. I arrived at his office later that morning prior to going to work. After some idle chit chat he asked why I had given myself a "B" for my class work. He was aware of my quality point deficit and wondered why I hadn't given myself an "A." I explained that I had never seen an "A" on any report card for four years and it might be just a little presumptuous that the first one would be self-administered. He said perhaps

I was being too hard on myself and, that if he had determined the grade, it would have been an "A." He went on that it must be my choice, that as the "teacher" in the class only I could make the proper grade determination. He couldn't change that "B"—and I wouldn't. He wished me luck and we said goodbye. It was unlikely we would ever see one another again.

About two weeks after my visit with Mr. Chenot, the mail came from Rockhurst that would have my grades for summer school. There was a sense of dread as I picked it up off the table. It would be yet another grade card of missed opportunities. Mr. Chenot had made it clear he would not change my grade, the only suspense was a likely "D" or a "C for charity" from Father Imbs. Finally I opened the envelope. My eye was immediately drawn to an "A" next to the course line for Introduction to Teaching. My heart was warmed that Mr. Chenot had overridden my "B." He was a pretty good guy, I thought. Having seen the "good news," my eyes gazed further down the page for the inevitable disappointment. I couldn't find the expected "D" or the unlikely "C," nor the early planned for "B" that would have satisfied the five quality points that was my wildest dream. Was there some unbelievable mistake made in academia? There was another "A." An "A" in the brain twisting History of the Industrial Revolution. My warmed heart was now overwhelmed. It wasn't that I had the five quality points one earns from an "A" and

18

a "B" but rather a sixth quality point from two "A's." A quality point to spare. An incalculable space somewhere beyond a "C" average! To this day in my life, it remains the most incredible sight I have ever seen.

I can only assume that Mr. Chenot, or someone, took the interest to find out why I was in that summer session. That he took my case to Father Imbs and to Father Weiss. That a decision was made that transcended academics. That whatever essential lessons intended to be imparted at Rockhurst had been accomplished. All would have known that I would soon find my way into a war that might never give me another chance to have my degree. I have often wondered, if had I assigned myself that "A" in Mr. Chenot's class, by my own hand or at his insistence,

if this story would end the same. It certainly wouldn't mean the same.

Two significant events were yet to unfold. A few weeks later in the mail I received my diploma, a Bachelor of Arts degree. A few months later in the mail I received my military orders for Vietnam.

Nearly forty years later when it comes to mind, it still warms my heart for just a second and finds my head perceptively shaking back and forth. I have been moderately successful in life. Should God allow me to hold some of the assets He has bestowed on me, when He calls me home, a sizable portion of what remains will find its way back to a small Jesuit college in the Midwest, all over one quality point.

A School on the Sand

Nancy Frees Fountain

Armed with five books, sunblock, and a bathing suit, I headed to Zihuatenejo, Mexico, for a full five days of rest and relaxation on the beach. Zihuatenejo, the sleepy fishing village and quiet sister to the more sophisticated Ixtapa.

Not long after arrival, I was stretched out on a palm mat, soaking up the last of the afternoon sun, a million miles from work, responsibility, complexities of any kind. Drifting in and out of sleep, I could feel the tension leaving my body and was soon one with the sound of the waves and the warm sand.

"Señora, Señora." A child's faint voice penetrated my peaceful state. I opened my eyes to find a young Mexican girl kneeling by my side with a plaid, plastic tote bag bulging with newspaper-wrapped objects for sale.

Carefully unwrapping one of the newspaper packages, the young girl placed a family of brightly colored onyx toucan birds on the palm of her hand. Father, mother, siblings, baby, all in descending order.

"Very nice, thank you," I said, "but I am not buying anything today because I just arrived and want to soak up these last rays of the day. Maybe another day."

Quickly, the young girl, now coming into better focus, began unwrapping many of the newspaper packages revealing different onyx animal families. Monkeys, rabbits, frogs, horses, ducks. Each family paraded on her palm, again in order of height. After each presentation, her big brown eyes searched my face for an expression of interest.

"What is your name, querida?"

"Juanita," she replied.

"My name is Nancy. How old are you?"

"I just turned eight."

I smiled at Juanita and told her that I liked the toucan family best and would buy this set to take home. It would remind me of her.

Next morning, I was on the beach early, securing a great spot under a thatched palm palapa. My big decision for the day would be which book to start. I didn't get far into the first book, when a familiar voice called from down the beach. It was Juanita. Running toward me, braids flying out behind her, same brown checked apron, orange flip-flops, and bulging plaid tote bag.

"Señora Nancy, good morning!"

"Juanita, how are you? Why aren't you in school?"

Juanita hung her head. She told me that she had gone to school for awhile, however, she was now needed to help in the family's market stall and to sell on the beach. Her brothers went to school. She had pleaded with her parents to let her go to school. They reminded her that girls did not need an education.

Awakened to the sad reality of this young girl's life, I explained to Juanita the importance of an education. I encouraged her to try to go back to school, if not now, at some time in the future. Education was a life-long pursuit. One could start school any time, but no one ever finished learning.

I asked Juanita if she could write her name. With sadness and shame she replied, "No."

"Do you want me to teach you to write your name?"

My pupil practiced the letters in her name. Over and over she wrote out the letters, finally stringing them together to spell, "Juanita." A huge smile punctuated her grand accomplishment.

"Let's celebrate!" I exclaimed. "Do you want a lemonade?"

I called the waiter over asking for two lemonades, one for me and one for my friend. The waiter was less than pleased, giving Juanita a menacing look. I repeated with a deliberate chilly edge, "Please be so kind as to bring my friend and me a lemonade."

Juanita gulped down her lemonade, carefully folded the paper with the final printing of "Juanita" on it, thanked me for teaching her to write her name, and ran down the beach stopping now and then to try to interest tourists in the contents of her tote bag.

Next morning, Juanita was waiting for me as I reached the beach palapas. I had imagined such and had brought pencils and paper.

"Bueños dias, Juanita! Are you ready for school on the beach?"

We practiced the alphabet and numbers one to ten. A few easy words, a couple of simple additions and subtractions. In the middle of our lesson, a break for lemonade served by our now openly irritated waiter. We finished our school lesson with a careful copying of the new words learned and math problems solved on a clean sheet of paper.

"Great job, Juanita! Tomorrow, school starts whenever you can come. I'll be waiting for you."

Amazingly, the books I brought to read did not capture my attention. My thoughts drifted towards issues of social justice, the importance of girls' education, the culture of poverty, inequities and oppression.

On the third morning, the sun was high overhead when I could see, far down the beach, a group of children running towards me. As they grew near, I could see that Juanita had interested two other young girls in joining our school on the sand.

For this day, I had purchased a writing tablet, pencils, and crayons. The new students were timid, yet eager to learn their letters and numbers. Sitting in a straight line, they practiced writing their names, letters, and simple words. Juanita, promoted to teacher's assistant, helped with the day's lesson.

The waiter brought over a tray with four glasses of lemonade, not happy about the increased number of guests.

I told Juanita and her friends that the next day would be the last day of school since I would be returning home. If they came again, I would have a surprise and something

very important I wanted to tell them.

The last morning, I gave my three students straw satchels filled with writing tablets, pencils, eraser, crayons, and books for beginning readers. I ordered some pan dulce and lemonade and asked the girls to listen to something very important.

I asked them to promise me they would keep learning to read and write. I encouraged them to ask their parents again if they could go back to school. If not, to make sure to ask for help with their learning. And to keep a dream of one day going to school, even if they had to wait until they were adults.

It was two years before I went back to Zihuatenejo again. I asked the "lemonade waiter" if he knew anything about Juanita. I wondered why she wasn't selling on the beach that morning.

"She is in school, Señora," he smiled.

"In helping others,
we shall help ourselves,
for whatever good we give out
completes the circle
and comes back to us."

FLORA EDWARDS

*"Too often we underestimate
the power of a touch, a smile,
a kind work, a listening ear,
an honest compliment,
or the smallest act of caring,
all of which have a potential
to turn a life around.
It's overwhelming to consider
the continuous opportunities
there are to make our love felt."*

LEO BUSCAGLIA

All You Need Is Love

Martha Daniel, Grade 6

My family and I had no idea it was coming. The thought of divorce petrified me and my little sister. When my parents broke the news that they were going to split up, I was terrified. Even though they weren't going to divorce, just live in separate houses, it was still scary.

After we had talked about the split for awhile, we went to see where my dad was going to live until they worked it all out. We went back home and I got a call from my friend Mabry Bolin. We never really got to see each other, so I was excited that she called. She was calling to see if I could spend the night, so later that night I went over to her house. After I had been there for about an hour, she asked if I was okay about the split. We talked about it for a while, and I felt a ton better. I later realized that this sleepover had been planned, but I was still glad we had it.

Mabry and her family had shown concern for me, and that made the difference. By showing a simple act of kindness, the Bolins gave me and my family the hope and the confidence to make it through the difficult time we were going through. My family received a lot of love during this time, and with that love we got through the split. My parents are now back together and happy as can be, thanks to the love they were shown by family and friends. The slightest act of showing you care can make a family's life together a whole lot better. And we got a lot of that love.

25

THE SLIGHTEST ACT OF SHOWING YOU CARE CAN MAKE A FAMILY'S LIFE TOGETHER A WHOLE LOT BETTER.

Alone in El Paso
Elena Cave

In 1970 I was alone in El Paso, Texas, thousands of miles away from home. My husband had first been stationed in Ft. Bliss and then had received orders to go to Vietnam. He left a few days before our son was born. After all, "The Army hasn't issued you a wife and baby" was what his Commanding Officer had said.

At twenty-two years old, with a newborn baby and a husband in Vietnam, I believed that I could manage everything successfully. I had always been called sensible and mature.

I was planning to drive to California to meet him there when he finished his tour of duty. As I was making my arrangements, I received a phone call from an old friend. Carmen and I had been friends since we were in sixth grade. We had bonded when we were assigned seats next to each other. Every afternoon we would walk home together and share our dreams.

I was excited about my future adventure, but a little apprehensive about the long road trip. These were the days before safe car seats for infants. I would be driving from El Paso to Los Angeles with a collapsible baby bed in the back seat. Ignorance and naiveté kept me going. I would wait in Texas until he was three months old.

There were many phone calls from Carmen and many long conversations about the trip. "Are you all right? Is the baby all right? Do you need anything?"

One Sunday she called and said that she didn't have time to talk too long and would call me for my birthday the next week. "I'll be home," I said and looked forward to the next call. My birthday was in early July and in late July I would be starting the drive to California.

Finally, it was my birthday and I wondered when the phone would ring. I was contemplating a trip to the market when the doorbell rang. I opened the door and couldn't believe what I saw. It was Carmen. She was carrying a large blue stuffed bear and a suitcase.

She said, "Happy Birthday." Later on she said she had decided that she couldn't let me have my adventure by myself and had always wanted to see Texas anyway. She stayed with me and we drove to California.

Through the years she has always been there for me. Now we've known each other over forty-five years. We still share many phone calls and remember that trip to California and how we were so young and invincible.

Always the Bridesmaid, Never......

Jill Pickett

I love stories that recount the ways in which we pay homage and say thank you to people who have been important in our lives while they are still alive to enjoy the acknowledgement.

While I was day-dreaming and standing in a long checkout line at a DSW Shoe Warehouse sale, I was told a rich story of giving and acknowledgment that gave me goose flesh and left me imagining that day many times afterwards. The story began when I heard a voice saying, "I can't believe I'm buying another pair of white satin shoes!" I shifted my focus from day-dreaming to the present moment and said, "Were you talking to me?"

She nodded and repeated, "I can't believe I am buying another pair of white satin shoes!" I noticed she was about thirty-two years old, a beautiful young woman with long blond hair, a big white smile, clear blue eyes, and a rather angelic looking suntanned face. She appeared to have a sweet sense of humor. I asked her how many pairs of satin shoes she already had. More than a dozen she answered. I asked why then was she buying more. "They are all the wrong color. These will need to be dyed a lime green," she elaborated.

She explained that she was going to be a bridesmaid for the twenty-fourth time in her young life. My mouth dropped open, she knew she had my attention, and she began to tell her story....

She had stood up as a bridesmaid for twenty-three girl friends over the past twelve years, remembering in detail without angst or whining the number of dresses, shoes, jewelry, hair appointments, dress fittings, and the cost. She said she had enjoyed them all, but was never able to let go of the dresses. So twenty-three bridesmaids' dresses were stored in the back of her seasonal clothes closet.

She said up to the twenty-third wedding, she was single and felt she personified the familiar saying, "Always a bridesmaid, never a bride!"

But two years ago she became engaged to the love of her life. Her friends wanted to throw her a couple's engagement party. She thought that was a lovely idea. The rest of the story she never expected.

Her friends knew she had stood in twenty-three weddings, always with a phenomenal attitude, and they knew no one else with such a history. They also knew she saved

27

every single bridesmaid's dress she'd ever bought and worn. So they arranged to secretly get all twenty-three dresses, and arranged for twenty-three female mannequins to be delivered to the elegant party room rented for the couple's engagement party.

The dresses became the backdrop, the décor, and the theme of the event. Each mannequin was perfectly coiffed and dressed in one of the bridesmaid dresses, which were all in perfect condition. All different colors, styles, and lengths. All representing twelve years of friendship, fun, memories, and a small fortune spent on dresses meant to be worn only once!

When the young couple walked into their engagement party, they saw first the twenty-three mannequins and bridesmaids' dresses. The young woman immediately knew what

they had done. She was stunned and richly amused at the creativity, the secrets kept, and her friends' proud faces. But when the young bride-to-be looked up at the stage where a sign hung with the theme of the evening she wept.

It said –

The Perfect Friend
Who was always a perfect bridesmaid
and is now
The Perfect Bride!

She had tears in her eyes as she stood in the DSW shoe store sharing her story with me, and then she looked down at the white satin shoes in the box she was holding, smiled and said, "At least these are on sale!"

Angels with Skin On

Russanne Kelley

It had been nine months since a diagnosis of breast cancer had altered my life's daily moments forever. Through the four months of increasingly stronger doses of chemo, I continued to work, only missing a day or two following a treatment when the sores in my mouth got too painful to swallow or talk and when nausea prevailed. Going into the mastectomy, I felt confident I would recover quickly and return to work in a week. I have always been a pathological optimist! God had other plans.

The discovery, following the operation, that the cancer had spread to my lymph nodes (five out of twenty infected), meant that extensive radiation would be needed. Trying to avoid a second reconstructive operation on my breast, I had arranged to have the expander inserted at the same time as the mastectomy. Now, with seven and a half weeks of radiation looming, that had to come out.

Still weak from the chemo sessions and now two operations, I felt my energy slipping away. At night, I would ask Jesus to put his cloak of healing around me and keep me safe until morning. I was afraid I wouldn't wake up. I stopped eating and only sipped warm water. My normal weight of 125 pounds slipped to 105. I dragged myself out of bed only to look around for a place to lie down. I had frequent panic attacks, usually precip-itated by a phone call or visit from my soon-to-be ex-husband of less than a year. It turned out that he didn't feel "in sickness and in health" included breast cancer, and his anger and resentment permeated all our conversations, leaving me exhausted and devastated.

It took a caring, experienced nurse at MD Anderson Cancer Center to look at me one day as I was going in for a treatment and to pull me aside afterwards and suggest I see a psychiatrist for my depression. My depression? I had no idea. I thought depression was for weak people. But, as I clung to her arm, tearfully looking into her reassuring eyes, I said "Yes, I will. Yes, whatever it takes to be me again."

She helped me make an appointment that day and, for the next several weeks, the psychiatrist and I worked to find the right anti-depressant medication for me. It was trial and error and, at times, very discouraging. I still felt weak and exhausted and too tired to go back to work.

By this time, my sick days and vacation days from work had all run out and I was looking at not continuing to receive a paycheck. This added to my worry and depression. My friends had moved me out of my husband's house months earlier, together with my dog and two cats, and the bills—medical, rent, vet, utilities—had begun to mount up.

That's when a miracle of love happened.

Friends from work, knowing my situation, donated much of their sick leave time—anonymously—to me so that I never had to be without a paycheck. When the HR director called to tell me the news, I cried from the beauty of it. It was such a relief, such a blessing! I shall never forget the kindness and generosity of those un-named friends—my angels with skin on.

Asita's Giving

Laura Biswas

My husband was born in Calcutta, India, and came to the United States as a small child. One of the stories I love to hear from him is about his paternal grandmother, who was a tiny woman (four feet ten inches!) who had a huge heart and keen sense of caring for others. Her name was Asita Boroni Biswas.

She was married very young to a man much older than herself who was the largest farmer in the tiny village where they lived in West Bengal. They were blessed to have enough resources to feed, educate and care for their large family of eleven children. The amazing story about Asita is that throughout her life, while raising her children and running this large household in rural India, she secretly managed to care for the poor in the village without even her family noticing. When she died, more than five hundred people from the village came to her funeral and countless ones came forward and revealed that she had quietly given food to them when in need. She would go to their homes to visit and purposely ask them for food to see if they had any. Once she saw they could not share anything or had very little, she would give them money or go home and have rice and other food delivered to their homes. What a beautiful heritage she left our family of generosity, caring for others and living in service.

31

Bonus Question, Bonus Friend

Samantha Night, Grade 6

Everybody either receives or gives random acts of kindness at least once in their lives, but there are some memories that just stay with us forever. I have one experience that I'll never forget. It's about one of my best friends, Allie, and I. It happened in history class, and it was a moment that displayed true friendship.

You see, that day in history we had a quiz with a bonus question on the back. Allie was the last person to get her quiz, and before she got it, another kid in our class asked her the bonus question. Without knowing that it was a question on the quiz, Allie said the answer out loud.

Our history teacher got so mad, and he made both Allie and the other kid go out of the room, after requesting to talk to them after class. When the bell rang, Allie and the other boy went into the room. All the other kids in the class went on their way, but I stuck around outside the door of the classroom. I could see Allie and our teacher talking; Allie was crying but I couldn't understand what she was saying. But then Allie's eye caught mine...she saw me through the door, even though our teacher didn't. I saw her smile through her tears. Fifteen minutes after the bell for class rang, Allie emerged from the room and immediately we hugged each other so hard.

"Thank you so much, Sam." she said, "I love you so much."

While this event may not be extremely significant at first glance, I'll never forget Allie's smile through the door at me, or our hug and the words she spoke. I know that Allie and I will be true friends forever, and I know that I'll love her like a sister until the end.

Bump a Nose

Connie Mendez (Chiquita)

I think those who have depression need to be picked up and taken somewhere to have fun and give them something to do. To be alone all day and sleep is not good. We need to be loved and need to fill a life.

My name is Connie Mendez. I was born in Houston, Texas, in the year 1953.

I came from a very poor family and to top it off there were nine children. But that was okay, because I always heard people saying that God gave us all a gift when he gave us life, so I am here for a reason. I am second to oldest and was severely abused physically and mentally by both parents. At the age of nine, I was super skinny because there were days I only ate one meal and others nothing at all. My hair was short and frizzy. I had real bad allergies so my nose was always running. I had to keep wiping it off with my hands. I have a big sister who is two years older than I am. She had only two dresses to wear and we both had to share them. She had this one green dress that I had to wear. It was too big and kept falling down from one side of my shoulders. I had a pair of red shoes that a neighbor gave me that were one size too small for my feet so they tore from the front. I had no socks so I used my father's socks. The socks stuck out of the front of the shoes making it look like the shoe had a tongue.

So I went to school looking like a clown. As I walked into the classroom, all the kids turned around to look at me and they all laughed at me. Some laughed so hard, they fell on the floor. Then my teacher said, "Leave her alone, she is mentally retarded."

Her words hurt me so much that I just wanted to die that day. I was thinking nobody loved me, not even God. I asked God, "Where is my gift? Did you forget me?"

At the age of eleven, I felt all alone in the world. I tried to commit suicide. No one knew why I did it and nobody asked me why. Life went on; I needed to be loved. But I goofed again. The first man who said I love you to me, I married. He didn't like to work and he beat me and my children. I had three kids and ended up raising them by myself. He left me. When my children grew up I was alone again.

Then one morning I woke up feeling very depressed. I asked God, "Why am I here? Where is my gift? Did you forget me?"

Then I had a flashback to my childhood years. I was crying and feeling very sad. Then

33

I said to myself, "You can't do anything right can you?" I said, "I just want to die. I can't take it any more. But before I do, I am going to take a walk one last time around the park."

As I was walking around the park with my head down and crying, I heard some voices of people laughing. I lifted up my head and saw some people walking into a small building and they looked very happy. I was thinking, why are they so happy? So I followed them into the building. There I saw a group of ladies laughing and having a good time sorting out boxes of clothing. This one lady who had a big smile came up to me and said, "Hi! I am Linda. What's your name?"

I said, "Connie."

34 Then she told me to come join them. "I really need all the help I can get. I need to sort out some clothing. I work for the Center for Faith and Health. My boss is Karen. We help out people in need of jobs, food and clothing.

"Will you please stay? We need you!" she asked.

"Sure," I said. The words "we need you" made me so happy my heart was beating fast with excitement. When we finished, I said goodbye to Linda.

And Linda said, "I'll see you tomorrow. Be sure to come back."

I walked out of there feeling like a new person. Those words: "we need you!"

Wow! They stayed in my mind. I was thinking, "Thank you, my God. All I want to do now is live because Linda needs me tomorrow."

AS I WALKED INTO THE CLASSROOM, ALL THE KIDS TURNED AROUND TO LOOK AT ME AND THEY ALL LAUGHED AT ME. SOME LAUGHED SO HARD, THEY FELL ON THE FLOOR. THEN MY TEACHER SAID, "LEAVE HER ALONE, SHE IS MENTALLY RETARDED."

When I came back, I joined in with the Fifth Ward seniors doing exercises with the nurse and also serving cake, coffee. Whenever I gave a senior a cup of coffee, they said, "Thank you. We need you! We are sure glad you're here!" Then they gave me a big hug. What they didn't know is their hugs and love kept me from committing suicide.

It was really the other way around. I needed them. I stopped trying to commit suicide and became a volunteer. The head of the seniors, Mama Rose, helped me to grow and I became part of their family. Never in my life had I ever received an award for anything. In 2002, I received my very first award for volunteering for the Center for Faith and Health.

They also raised funds for me to go to clown school where I graduated as a clown. My clown name is Chiquita. And now I know it's true. God does love me and he did not forget me. He did give me a gift. He gives us all a gift. Now I understand why all the kids laughed at me in school. God gave me the gift of making people laugh.

I'm not weird. I'm gifted. Thank you, God, and all the people who volunteer. Thank you for my gift.

Giving your gifts to others is,
in a very real sense, giving to yourself.
You may think you are giving to others,
but you are really giving yourself a chance
to be your best. You're giving yourself
a chance to live your values, express your
talents, and share your love. You're giving
yourself a chance to experience
yourself making a meaningful difference
and to feel fully alive in the process.

LAWRENCE BODH

*"Giving connects two people,
the giver and the receiver,
and this connection gives birth
to a new sense of belonging."*

DEEPAK CHOPRA

By the Hand of a Child

Quynh-Anh McMahan

One summer while in college, I decided to expand my horizons and work as a volunteer counselor for a camp serving children living with HIV/AIDS. I had some hesitations because, although I'd volunteered with homeless children, low income families, and other vulnerable populations, I had limited knowledge of what it was like to be affected by this tragic disease. I definitely felt a bit out of my comfort zone.

Once on the campgrounds, I attended orientation, then the buses of kids showed up, and cabin assignments were made. I had been assigned to the "Girls, Aged 8-10" group. As the children filed in to the cabin, I suddenly felt a sense of panic: "Why was I here?...What could I offer?...Would they like me?...What if I said something wrong?...Or worse, what if something happened to one of these girls under my care?"

I was thankful that the kids were oblivious to the thoughts swimming around my head, as they were busy settling in. I immediately noticed some differences among my group of girls. Some had been to the camp before, had known one another and were energetically chatting it up, while others sat on the edges of the group and observed. Some had nicely packed luggage sitting on their beds, while others came in with their small amount of clothing stuffed in a garbage bag.

One of the new campers without luggage took a bed in the far corner of the cabin. I'd already sensed that this little girl had "four strikes" against her: she was poor, she was African-American, she was a girl, and she had been infected with HIV. She was eight and her name was CeCe. With a round, cherubic face and lovely braided hair, she appeared shy, though had an endless supply of smiles. As the kids began to line up for the day of activities ahead of us, CeCe walked up and latched onto my hand.

We remained at each other's hips the rest of the week. As we were both new to the camp, we got lost finding our way around the grounds—where was the arts and crafts building, and the dining hall, and the all-important swimming pool? We were both learning our way around together.

During the course of that first day, I found the group of campers to be like any other kids—bubbly, curious, whiny, fun-loving, even a bit loud and rowdy at times. But I

One of the new campers took a bed in the far corner of the cabin.
I sensed that this little girl had "four strikes" against her:
she was poor, she was African-American, she was a girl,
and she had been infected with HIV.

also observed that these children had additional life burdens that their "healthy" peers did not have: each lined up for medications, shots and other unpleasant procedures, several times a day for some. It was heartbreaking to see what their small bodies had to endure.

Mid-week, as our cabin was winding down into our evening routine, I made sure that all the girls had brushed their teeth, combed their hair, put on their PJs and generally quieted down (giggling seemed to be a specialty of my campers). When I'd noticed most were drifting off to dreamland, I walked over to my bed, ready for the comforts of sleep myself.

There I found a lovely sign made of construction paper waiting for me. In child-like scrawl, it was heavily decorated with hearts and smiley faces and read, "I love you. Love CeCe". Seeing this almost made my heart stop, as I suddenly realized that though my intention in coming to this camp was to give my time, energy and comfort to these children, I had indeed been abundantly blessed by the hope, friendship and acts of kindness extended to me by CeCe and so many like her in my moments of insecurity and self-doubt.

This experience reinforced for me that service is a reciprocal act, with no clear "givers and receivers," but with spirits who are willing to give up their "selfs" to sustain what is good, pure and just about humanity.

Changing My Life

André Gras, Grade 6

There have been acts of kindness, great and small, from friends, family, and teachers alike. This one changed my thoughts about people, my prejudices, and pretty much my life. It was an act of kindness from strangers who then became friends. It started in Kindergarten.

I was all alone in a new school and it was the first day. I didn't know anybody and I didn't care. I was a solitary kid, except for in my old school. Even then, I only had three friends. One was Brian, who now goes to Lanier Middle School; another was Allison, who still goes to the same school, and the last, Jack, who left to live in Iceland for five years. I haven't seen him since. I knew I was going to have to make friends sometime, but I was way too shy. I would not talk to anyone and no one would talk to me. That's how it went for pretty much the first day; until it came to Recess.

This, even though I didn't know it, would change my life. I walked out sullen and depressed. I was mad at myself for being so stupid to change schools. I was just a copycat. I only wanted to go to this school because my older brother went there. Well anyway, I was walking to recess disheartened and I sat on a bench. I watched the other kids play, but I noticed two kids with dirty blond hair who looked a lot alike. I thought they were

brothers, because they hung around the whole recess together. I didn't know it but they noticed me sitting on the bench dejected.

They walked over and simultaneously said, "You wanna play with us?" I agreed warily. I thought they were playing a joke on me. I was wrong. The second thing I said to them was if they were brothers. They laughed and cheerfully said, "No." I was kind of uneasy around people having so much fun on their first day. I came to like these two blond kids, and I knew when I had agreed to play with them my life would change.

Being with them changed my prejudice about people and my opinions on things. These kids changed my life. In a good way.

Food for Body and Soul

Katy Gill

It is not unusual for friends to ask how they can help when a family is coping with illness. Though many offer their assistance, it is those who take initiative and then provide help with quiet grace that makes their giving extraordinary.

Such was the case when my mother was in the final stage of a chronic illness. Mother was in intensive care for a month before we brought her home for hospice care (yet another grace). My father, sister, and I spent as much time with her as possible leaving little or no opportunity to run errands or prepare meals. We were especially concerned about my elderly father who needed to maintain his own health and strength (and who, it should be noted, was used to eating regularly each day, and though he has always been slim, eating with relish).

My dear friends and colleagues rallied. I knew something was "cooking" when one asked if Daddy or I had any foods we could not eat or did not like. Without much fanfare, an ice chest appeared at my front door, and every night when I got home weary and sad, dinner was waiting for me. At the same time, dinner was delivered to my dad each evening. Dining, instead of being alone, actually became a good part of the day for him as many of my friends took time to visit with him when they brought food. He looked forward to their company, and to the delicious suppers. So much was given us, we had to ask our chefs to slow down a bit. The service was also offered to my sister and her family, but her circle of friends was taking good care of them.

I'm not sure words can ever adequately express what a kind and thoughtful gesture this was. There is such comfort in food and friendship, and the dinners brought to us were sustenance for our souls as well as for our bodies.

40

Gift from a Twin

Tommy C., Grade 6

There are many people who have been kind to me in my life. One person in particular has helped me the most (excluding parents). She is my Aunt Alexa, who is my mom's twin sister.

Aunt Alexa is nice to me all the time but there was one particular moment when she was nice at a very hard time. It was around half a year ago just before school started. My mom was sick in the hospital with cancer. She was getting in worse and worse condition so all my relatives came down to Houston. Aunt Alexa was the first to get here and she met Betsy, Robby, my dad, and I in the hospital. We were very upset because our mom could barely sit up or speak to us. When I started crying, Aunt Alexa comforted me; we sat together and prayed. I am really glad she did this because it made me feel a lot better. A little while later my mom died and Aunt Alexa sat with us and hugged us really tight. Then we drove home. Once home the other relatives arrived. She stayed with us for a week to help comfort us and get things done.

She really helped us out. She helped us to stay positive and get out of the house by taking us to restaurants and stores. Also, she got me to keep reading my summer reading book and buying more uniform clothes and school supplies so I would be ready for school. We really wouldn't have made it through the summer without her love and help.

41

Giving Transcends Language

Loren Lewis

Back in the day when you could actually meet passengers at the gate, I was awaiting the arrival of a friend at LAX when I noticed a woman holding a very young baby.

Having just become an aunt and desperately missing my nephew who lived in Ohio, I approached her. It quickly became apparent that she spoke no English, but we somehow communicated, and as they floated by one by one I soon met her six other children.

The war in Vietnam had recently ended and they were coming to rebuild their lives with her brother in Texas. Unfortunately, their connecting flight was cancelled and there wasn't another until the next day. So with seven children, no money, no accommodations, no English and no food, they were planning to spend the night at the airport. This was unacceptable; I would take them home with me if I had to, but first I addressed the Gate Agent. He explained that he was sorry, but there just wasn't another flight. I said, "What about other airlines?" Miraculously, there was one leaving in an hour, and using their tickets he was able to book them, but not before they were all given food vouchers to sustain them until then. I hurriedly phoned their relatives with the new itinerary (no cell phones in those days)

and left only after I saw them fed and ready to board.

I really didn't do much, but in letters I later received I learned how grateful they were, referring to me as their "American Mother." We kept in touch for a while, and I sent items I thought they could use, but having moved fourteen times since then we eventually, and unfortunately, lost touch.

Speaking with people throughout the world where he's traveled much of his life doing conflict resolution, Marshall Rosenberg, founder of Non-Violent Communication says, "Universally, there's no better game than contributing to the well being of another." This family may have felt that I helped them, but they probably have no idea how they touched my heart and enriched my life, and how grateful I am to have been given the opportunity.

Good Grief

Dale Shaughnessy

Gifts can come in all sorts of packages and they may surface when you least expect them. They come in life... or in death. We must be open to receiving them. They must not remain unwrapped.

I received a gift from my father, but not in the way you or he would expect. Don't get me wrong; my father was hugely generous. He loved to shop, he loved to pick out cards, and most of all, he loved to give gifts, usually ceremoniously and with great celebration! It wasn't always a material item. It could be a trip, a sporting endeavor, an educational adventure, a down payment on a dream. But it was always expensive. He equated money with success. That is why he worked so hard, why he was so driven, why he worked himself to death.

My father gave me an endless amount of gifts; the most noteworthy wrapped in silver, the lining of a bleak and bleary, black cloud. My father's gift grew from his death, like a bud in a barren flower bed. My gift was grief and subsequent counseling. My counselor helped me identify the pain that hovered over me, helped me embrace my fears of death and loss. In doing so, I learned a lot about myself, my values, my priorities. I set out on a new path, where I set the boundaries, where clarity takes the place of cloudiness, where there is

a gentle breeze rather than a gale force wind. A feeling of well being is in the air.

Good grief is my silver-packaged gift from my dad. He would be pleased, I think, at how I utilized it. No squandering or carelessness, rather used with introspection and thoughtfulness. With more time and less financial demands, new interests, new people, new coursework have emerged. Fate has brought some old contacts back into play. My gift has allowed me to reinvent myself. I have become a better mother, a better daughter. My father would like that. I have become a better reader and a better writer, too. He would be happy about that as well, for he was a lover of the printed word. That's another gift I inherited from him. But that's another story and perhaps chapter in my life.

43

The Harvest of My Father's Soul

Maggie Carlton

When I met Father John, I was stunned by the remarkable similarities he shared with my dear Father Chatham. Father John had the same robust stature, gentle hands, soft brown eyes and warm smile.

The intensive-care doctors were shocked when my "comatose" father communicated that I should contact the bishop's office and locate Father John. My father had never met this spiritual man but somehow knew he needed to connect with him.

In the sweltering August Mississippi heat I had just set up my lemonade stand under a gigantic magnolia tree when my first customer arrived. He was a robust stranger dressed in black except for his white collar. He approached me with five cents in hand and asked for a "double". His massive demeanor initially startled me, but as he handed over his payment, I noticed his gentle hands, soft brown eyes and divine smile. I knew right away he was a caring man.

It was 1955, I was five years old and we had just moved to Jackson, Mississippi. Our family consisted of one mother, one father and five children. Three more kids came later and we referred to them as "the little girls." We also had two Dobermans, many of their puppies and God only knows how many cats, kittens and one parakeet who loved to poop on our blonde curly hair.

The purpose of this stranger's visit was to welcome our family to the community and invite us to attend Mass at his church. Father Josiah Chatham was the founder and pastor of Saint Richard's Catholic Church and soon became my favorite person in the world. Amazingly, he also became my atheist father's best friend. I believe that the intelligence of these two men brought them together and held their friendship intact despite their spiritual disparity. Decades later, I learned how this holy man would influence my father's spiritual destiny.

Soon after Father Chatham came into our lives, my mother decided our entire family should become Catholic, with the exception of my atheist father. Daddy was a scientist by profession, and he made it perfectly clear that he did not believe in God. He simply would not accept the concept of Christianity, Eternity or a Higher Being. His insistence was profoundly confusing to this five-year-old girl who had just begun to embrace Christianity.

After several spirit-filled meetings with Father Chatham, Mom took all five of her children to St. Richard's and Father Chatham

44

reverently baptized us on a heaven-sent Sunday afternoon. Our neighbors, Mr. and Mrs. Fleck were our godparents. This was a blessed day and we celebrated our newly sanctified lives at home with cake and ice cream. Just hours after the big event, my new godparents, along with Father Chatham, "saved my life" as the three of them retrieved my tiny, new, red Radio Flyer tricycle and my hysterical muddy self, still dressed in my crisp white organdy baptism dress, from the drainage ditch in front of their home. In a state of excitement from the day's activities, I peddled so fast that I slipped off the sidewalk and tumbled into a three-foot deep ravine that seemed like the Grand Canyon. I can still recall the lavender scent of Mrs. Fleck and the gentle hands of Mr. Fleck and Father Chatham as they so lovingly rescued me from that hellhole.

We never knew when Father Chatham would surprise us with a visit. He loved to enjoy an ice-cold beer, a bologna sandwich or a bowl of corn flakes while engaging in intellectual banter with my father. Whenever I knew that he was coming, I would curl up and hide on the creaky front porch swing and wait for him. He approached the steps and I would leap out of the swing, jump into his huge arms, embraced in one of his great big hugs. He always acted astonished, then sat down beside me and we would talk and swing as high and fast as we could until my father came outside and stole him away from me. He treated all of us kids with such respect and made us feel special. My mother loved Father Chatham because he brought peace to our always-chaotic lives.

Santa brought me, on our first Christmas in our new Mississippi home, the present that I got on my knees and prayed for every night—a miniature, ultra-modern, 100-watt light-bulb-activated Betty Crocker oven! I could hardly wait to create miniature cakes and cookies and proudly serve them to Father Chatham on his frequent visits. With exaggerated expressions of gastronomical nirvana he gobbled up each and every morsel as if he was starving for my delectable treats. He made me feel like the best little cook on the planet.

When I was seven years old, my family moved to Texas. It was difficult to leave Mississippi and our beloved Father Chatham. For many years after the move, he took the time to answer my letters and often traveled to the Lone Star State to visit our family. His inspiration magnified my faith in God and influenced my innocent soul. I wanted to be the best person I could be and to this day, I continue to be inspired by this man.

In the mid-1980s, my parents drove to Mississippi to pay their final respects to Father Chatham. By this time he had achieved the revered title of Monsignor and was wheelchair-bound, suffering from muscular dystrophy. He died three years later. He was a great scholar, liturgist and compassionate pastor. His goodness touched many, many souls. His death broke countless hearts, including my father's and mine.

Years later, I vacationed in Scotland at the castle home of friends who were renewing their wedding vows. Their friend from childhood, Father John, whose parish was in Houston, officiated the blessing in a lovely ceremony at their castle. Ironically, at this time, Houston was also my home. During my visit, Father John and I had many opportunities to get to know one another and we developed a bond that would dramatically influence where my father spent eternity! (At least I believe this to be the case.)

45

When I met Father John, I was stunned by the remarkable similarities he shared with my dear Father Chatham. Father John had the same robust stature, gentle hands, soft brown eyes and warm smile. I shared with him the history of my friendship with Father Chatham. As we became more acquainted, I continued to be amazed by this man who took me back in time. My week in Scotland flew by as I enjoyed each conversation, his intelligence and kindheartedness.

Upon returning to Houston I learned that my father was hospitalized with a shocking diagnosis of bone cancer. I immediately rushed to his hospital bed. He had always been an avid reader who loved travel and dreamed of faraway places. He admired the culture of the Scottish people, the beauty of hills and brilliant flowers that filled meadow after meadow. But Scotland was a destination that never happened for him. As I described to him in great detail the beauty of the countryside and my new friendship with Father John, I shared the many photos that I brought home. Immediately, it became evident that it was not just I who was fascinated by the likeness of the two priests. Even in his very weak state, my father became quite animated and emotional as I described similarities—both physical demeanor and character of each beloved man. It was uplifting to see my dying father so "alive" with an enthusiasm that I could not define.

Prior to my father's unexpected illness, my brothers, sisters and I planned an elaborate fiftieth wedding anniversary party for our parents. The likelihood of that celebration became grim as we accepted our father's imminent death. A few days after my return from Scotland, Daddy had a massive stroke and in the middle of the night, I was called to the hospital to find him in the intensive care unit in a dreadful state. My family was scattered about Texas, but the doctors insisted that someone make immediate decisions regarding necessary medical procedures. After numerous phone calls to my family, I had no idea what to do until they arrived the following morning.

The intensive-care doctors were shocked when my "comatose" father communicated that I should contact the bishop's office and locate Father John. My father had never met this spiritual man but somehow knew he needed to connect with him. I located Father John's parish and learned that he had just left Scotland and was en route to Houston.

Immediately upon his arrival in Houston, a representative from his parish met Father John at the airport and rushed him to the hospital where my father was barely clinging to life. When Father John approached my father's bedside, I saw life in my father's eyes for a brief moment. Father John took my father's hand and respectfully asked if he wished to receive his Last Rights. A subtle nod answered the question. Father John proceeded by anointing my father's forehead with holy oil, took my hands as we prayed together. Then Father John placed his gentle hands on my father and looked at me with his tender, soft brown eyes. My memory immediately flooded with the recollection of my first encounter with Father Chatham under the magnolia tree, his nickel in hand, anticipating the ice cold lemonade refreshment that would change our lives. As I brought myself back to reality, Father John's kind smile assured me that my father was on his way to heaven. He died the next day, at home, with our family by his side.

In the early years, Father Chatham sowed the seeds of faith in my father's life. In the end, Father John was sent to harvest these seeds to save one man's soul.

J.C.'s Messages

Natali Chavez

One of the greatest changes of my life was going to college 2,000 miles away from home in a place where I did not know a single person.

When I started thinking to which colleges I wanted to apply, I decided to go somewhere far away from home due to my innate sense of adventure.

I wanted to see new places and meet new people. I applied to the University of Notre Dame, and when I received my acceptance letter, I was thrilled to know I would be able to have such an experience. I was aware that attending school in South Bend, Indiana, would be difficult since my life would be completely different from what I was accustomed. Nonetheless, I accepted the fact that I would be completely on my own in a strange place, and tried to prepare myself to leave my family and friends.

Although I had thought thoroughly about the separation, arriving at school was more overwhelming than I had anticipated. The realization of this new challenge I was taking on hit me from the very first moment I set foot on campus. Fortunately, I was lucky enough to have a great friend who supported me through it all. The very first night, my best friend, J.C., sent me a text message to make sure I had arrived safely. I told him I was somewhat overwhelmed by being in a new place with so many strangers surrounding me. He reassured me that I would feel at home in no time, and that I would make lots of friends, and I would do fine in all my classes.

For the entire month after I arrived at Notre Dame, he would call me at least twice a week. He sent me a card, and a letter with pictures of the last time we went out. It is funny how important receiving mail becomes when you are in college. One of my most memorable moments, however, was when I woke up one morning and read a text message he sent me earlier saying, "Good morning, hope you have a wonderful day." It was a simple gesture but it meant a lot to me. It brightened up my morning and left a smile on my face for the rest of the day.

J.C.'s constant support and kind words made my transition to college so much easier. He always reminded me there were people who loved me, and that I was capable of doing anything. Every single gesture, no matter how small, made a world of difference to me. I truly believe it is the simplest actions that mean the most and show a person how much you care.

John and Johnny

Cynthia Peacock

I grew up next door to a family who had a child with mental retardation. I don't really remember any aspect of my childhood without John. At the time my sister, brother and I were in grade school, John was in his adolescent years.

If you had asked me when I was a child, how old John was, I probably would of said, "old like my parents," but of course looking back he probably was only eighteen or nineteen. Even back then, John's mother was a typical parent of a special needs child, an advocate, always fighting for the rights of her son and making sure he got all of the benefits due him. Because of her son, she ended up working for the Mental Health Mental Retardation Association. John's mother didn't stop there. Not only did she work for an agency that devoted its resources to the disabled, but she was consistently bringing home special needs children for the weekend from a nursing home in our community.

All the kids in the neighborhood knew and loved John. He was never without a neighborhood kid holding on to his hand or sharing a ride on his bike. He had a collection of keys that was mesmerizing to a child, and of course he was always ready to show them on request. We use to take turns having John give us rides in his wheelbarrow and if we wanted to ride our bikes down to the corner store, the parents in the neighborhood would only allow it if John rode with us. I guess the parents thought having an adult figure with us would protect us. Looking back on it, I think we were John's protectors. We never allowed anyone to tease him or call him names. Of course as a kid, you would always protect your friend, and he was our friend.

A special treat for all of the kids in the neighborhood was when John's mother would bring home a young boy who had cerebral palsy and was in a wheelchair. His name was Johnny and he was twelve or thirteen years old at the time. We didn't see him as a handicapped child but a kid who had a neat form of transportation that we could play with. I can remember numerous times when my mother came out of the house yelling at all of us to be careful with him as we raced him up and down the street in his wheelchair, and, of course, quite a few of us were hanging

49

on to the wheelchair as it spiraled out of control down the dirt road. In our neighborhood if we played baseball we had to include everyone, even the little ones who couldn't run. The rule was if my five-year-old brother made contact with the ball, he got to run the bases in Johnny's lap. I don't think Johnny ever had a better time than when he was being pushed around the bases in his wheelchair, his arms flailing, laughing, and my brother holding on to him for dear life.

As I grew up with both John and Johnny, my friendship with them continued. I would come home from nursing school and John would be sitting on the porch waiting for me because, like any neighborhood, everyone knew when the prodigal son or daughter was due home from college. He would immediately race over to the car and request a car ride with me. The bags of dirty laundry wouldn't even make it out of the car as John and I rode around town. We would have to stop and admire the new construction that was going on, or take a ride over to see Johnny. It never was a chore for me to spend that time with John or Johnny; it came naturally to me because they were essentially part of my family.

Johnny's mother was extremely ill one weekend when I came home to visit my parents. My mother insisted that I visit with her because she wasn't expected to live out the week. I remember going over to the house and being led into the bedroom where she laid pale and having problems breathing. She asked that I sit next to the bed and she held my hand. She inquired about my nursing career and if I enjoyed what I was doing. I

had just hired on as a visiting nurse and told her stories of the patients that I took care of in their homes. She reminded me of a promise that I made to her as a child. The promise was that I would grow up and get a job taking care of people like Johnny and John. She asked me if I would be able to keep that promise. At that time, with her so sick, I would have promised her anything just to see the joy on her face that she got from me telling her I was still committed to that promise. Little did I realize that the promise would come full-circle back to me.

Twenty-five years later I am now a physician and I am in my third year of running a clinic for adolescent and young adults with chronic childhood illnesses. I see patients with sickle cell disease, congenital heart disease, Down syndrome, spina bifida and, of course, mental retardation and cerebral palsy. I didn't really plan this, nor did I think I would have fulfilled the dream of a dying old lady. Some people would call it fate or destiny; others would see it as karma or divine intervention. My mother, who is a religious woman, would say God had something to do with it. I am not sure what forces in nature made the reality of my clinic happen, other than maybe it was the ride in the wheelchair with Johnny down a dirt road on a sunny summer day or maybe it was all the car rides around town with John and watching his excitement seeing all the new construction. Maybe I did it just for them.

"We yearn—in our deepest hearts—
not to take but to give,
and in that giving to deeply receive."

MARC GAFNI

"*And while it takes courage*
to achieve greatness, it takes more
courage to find fulfillment in being ordinary.
For the joys that last have little
relationship to achievement, to standing one
step higher on the victory platform.
What is the adventure in being ordinary?
It is daring to love just for the pleasure of
giving it away. It is venturing to give
new life and to nurture it to maturity.
It is working hard for the pure joy
of being tired at the end of the day.
It is caring and sharing
and giving and loving …"

MARILYN THOMSEN

Letter to the Editor

Steve Barnhill

I read with interest your op-ed piece this morning on the state of the college football coaching, whose practitioners, not unlike their employers, show diminishing respect for signed contracts, less regard for personal commitments, and no appreciation at all for that ethereal but potent energy we call loyalty, a force that binds us to a course of action because of the special value we place on people apart from ourselves.

As I was reading your paper, a notable story was unfolding here in Houston. Coaches could take a lesson from it. The story reminds me that while all are not loyal, neither is all lost.

To appreciate the story, I must take you back almost a year to the day that my good friend Marie was approached by her colleague, Ann, about one of her life goals —to train for and finish a marathon. "My primary motivation for this crazy pursuit is to honor my husband, who has muscular dystrophy," Ann told Marie. "I'd like to ask people to pledge money and, that way, raise funds for the Muscular Dystrophy Association. But I've never run a long race and have no idea how to make this happen!"

At that moment, Marie grabbed Ann's hands, looked in her eyes, and said with conviction, "I have no doubt you have it in you to do this, and I will be right by your side along the way."

Marie was a veteran of eight marathons. These days, however, she was comfortably retired from competition, tending to two gregarious daughters and a college-student son, a demanding job, a full load of coursework leading to her master's degree, and a three-bedroom home. Suddenly her life was to get busier—and richer.

She proceeded to train with Ann, running at her side as both women built strength and stamina. Early morning and late nights they ran together, abiding heat, rain and cold, developing endurance and forging a relationship unique in each of their lives.

Then came the complication.

Marie, who lived in Texas, was enrolled in a master's program at a well-known university in another city. As chance would have it, the Sunday of the marathon she was supposed to be in class. In so many words, she needed a "walk" so she could run. This ought to be easy, she thought. Who wouldn't understand?

53

Marie confidently met with her faculty leaders to inform them that she'd need to be absent on Sunday, January 14, to run the marathon with her friend.

Their response was as prompt as it was unexpected. If she chose to miss class, they said, Marie would risk not graduating. Her attendance in every class was mandatory.

Dare Marie risk not graduating merely to keep her commitment? Could she face working hard for two years, flying to another city for classes several days every month, paying big tuition fees, laboring night upon night to complete her coursework on the degree she had long aspired to own—just to run another painful marathon? Heck, she'd been there and done that many times. She had nothing to prove. And wasn't Ann, a grown woman, now able to run the race alone? Yes to all questions. But Marie had made a promise to Ann, and to Marie, promises were made to be kept.

So, shortly after midnight on Sunday, January 14, the day of the race, having attended her Friday and Saturday but not her Sunday classes, Marie forsook her studies and boarded a red-eye to Houston, landing at 6:00 A.M. in the morning.

Ignoring her fatigue, Marie then drove directly home to don her running clothes. By pre-arrangement, her youngest daughter was waiting. Marie jumped into her aging Toyota, her daughter now at the wheel, and the two hurried across town to Rice University where, at mile eleven, Marie stepped onto University Boulevard and joined Ann.

Stride for stride, Marie then paced her friend on the meandering roads toward the realization of a goal that lay 26 miles and 385 yards from the marathon's starting mark.

Nearing the finish, Marie dropped back and urged Ann to run ahead and "make sure you run in the middle of the street, because that way you'll get a good picture of yourself crossing the finish line!"

Ann completed the race in 5:26:57, and Marie followed shortly thereafter. As she crossed the line, Marie's graduation was in question, but her integrity was intact.

Both women received shiny finisher's medals and proceeded to the "Reunion Area." There Ann met her husband, who was waiting with a satisfied smile and a bouquet of roses. She draped the medal around his neck, saying, "This was as much your race as it was mine."

"It was a scene I'll never forget," recalls Marie. "Ann is simply wonderful."

Yes, Ann is wonderful. So is her loyal running buddy. And so is a commitment that is fulfilled at the risk of personal cost.

In my opinion, Marie and Ann, who raised over $3,600 for MDA, could teach a lesson to some academicians. They could certainly take some college coach "to school." Their example provides a lesson for the rest of us, too. The next time we need someone to help us realize an improbable dream, we might consider looking past the beefy young man filled with rah-rah and fired by ambition. Better that we count on a petite, unassuming, overworked, 50-something mom whose word is her bond.

Based on what I've witnessed, she'll be the one who goes the distance with us.

Listening to Ms. T

Vicki Kirchhoff

Sometimes when you think you're seeking one thing, something else develops and becomes more beneficial than your original intentions.

A few years ago, I did some volunteer work at an assisted-living facility. My motive was to find two to four elderly ladies who had little or no family to visit them and maybe I could make them feel a little better with a touch of makeup, a new hairdo, polish their nails, etc. When discussing the candidates for me to select from with the manager in charge of that floor, she mentioned one lady in particular (Ms. T) who did have some family who visited occasionally. However, Ms. T was the most difficult and ornery resident they had ever had and she was sure neither I nor anyone would spend time with her. I was told that Ms. T had become almost totally blind in the last year or two and had been living by herself. Well, for some reason, I was intrigued hearing about Ms. T and surprisingly to me, I wanted to make an attempt at meeting her and see what would happen.

Once we were at Ms. T's door outside her room, I thought to myself, What in the world was I going to say to her and how was I going to convince her that all I wanted to do was be a friend to her? We entered the room and immediately I was challenged with her rough talk and argumentative statements, asking who I was and why I was there. However, something inside of me said that I needed to be there. The manager talked to Ms. T a while and then I began to get closer to her bedside and joined in the conversation. Ms. T made a few more snide remarks and then for some reason, she began to change her tone and proceeded to speak as if she had something to tell me. The manager then realized that Ms. T was allowing me to stay in her room for the time being and so we were left by ourselves.

From that afternoon and for the next two months, I began a journey with Ms. T that has added a new dimension in my comprehension. She allowed me to become a part of her newly created make-believe world of friends that she developed in her new world of darkness. Ms. T went into great detail to explain to me each time I visited all about her new friends and the day to day occurrences. It was a world that no one could imagine in our world of day and night. She could visualize the sun and moon, and all the pleasures of sight that we take for granted. Her fantasy friends brought her their happiness, sorrows, gossip, and everything

55

When discussing the candidates for me to select from,

the manager mentioned one lady, Ms. T, who was

the most difficult and ornery resident they had ever had.

I was told that Ms. T had become almost totally blind

and had been living by herself. Well, for some reason,

I wanted to make an attempt at meeting her.

57

else that good friends share. I remember that I could not wait to go visit Ms. T each week to find out the latest news with her friends. It was a novel in the making.

Ms. T had a remarkable sense of humor as well as a "salty" flair in her vocabulary. She seemed so pleased that someone was interested in taking the time to hear all about her new life with friends who seemed real to her and not judge her for what seemed insane to others. This was her way of coping with the disease that left her blind. This lady trusted me enough to share secrets that perhaps no one else could understand.

Little did I realize that for the brief moment in time with this lady, I would receive wisdom, purpose, joy and fulfillment that will enrich my life forever. When she passed away, the facility notified me and I received the most touching thank you letter from Ms. T's children. They had heard about a lady who came to visit each week and Ms. T wasn't quite sure why I was there, but she missed me when I was gone. Actually, I am the one who felt a void for quite a few months after she passed, but I know I was sent to her to share an extraordinary bonding that will never be duplicated.

Little Things

Jane Labanowski, Grade 6

Sometimes little things can make a person feel good, like someone popular saying hi to someone who is, well, not so popular; or someone standing up to a bully for the little kid who's being picked on.

These little things can make a person feel so good. The thing is most of the time, it is so easy for the person doing the kind thing to do it. An example of my theory is that this year I am at a new school. Although it's not hard for me to make new friends, it was hard for me to leave my old school, my comfort zone, and start all over. In about the beginning of the year, one of my best friends got invited to a sleepover and I wasn't invited, and I found out about it. I know, I know, not a very big deal, but I was a little disappointed and felt a little rejected. Then that night, I got a call from the person holding the sleepover inviting me to come, too. I was really excited and although it was just a little, tiny, easy thing to do, it made me feel great! This act gave me a speck of confidence that had definitely not been there before the invitation, and helped me make new friends and get comfortable at my new school. My point is that I am sure it wasn't hard to give me an invitation but it made me feel so good.

Every day you should try to do those little things that make people feel good because you might be the next person to want something little to happen to you.

Midnight Memory

Emily Diaz, Grade 6

Have you ever felt that sinking feeling in your chest, where you can't believe what just happened, why it has, and what you did to deserve it? It's not a very good feeling, right? It's almost like you are falling. As you are getting nearer and nearer to the ground, you are starting to get faster and faster, almost like "Alice in Wonderland" when she was falling down the secret burrow to find the rabbit.

I have in truth had an experience like this. Only I was six and it was not all just a dream. It happened while I was sleeping. I had just gone through my regular routine for the night, eating dinner, brushing my teeth, kissing daddy goodnight and leading mommy into my room to read the book that I had wanted to read every night since my cousin, Madeleine, had shown it to me. Then kiss mommy right before I was about to go to sleep. Only that night, everything went off schedule. I was just dozing off when daddy walked into my room. I asked why he was there, because I had already kissed him goodnight. He then said that he had some bad news. Actually, more like incomprehensibly horrible news for a little girl of only six. Just those ten little words made a huge impact in my life in a matter of minutes. Trembling, he walked over to my bed.

"Your cousins and uncle died in a car crash tonight," my dad whispered in my ear as if

to hold it in so I wouldn't let it out. I truthfully couldn't blame him. I did want to let it out. Let it out of my head. Out of my life. Just those ten words.

I later found myself in a limo. But it wasn't leading my family to a dinner party, no. Instead it was leading us to a much worse occasion. A funeral. It seemed like forever until it was finally over. I just wanted to jump right out of my seat and leave. Even for a six-year-old, it was hard. I could hear my aunt crying from a distance and then hear my mom's comforting yet stable voice. That meant that it was time to leave Dallas. My mom wanted my aunt, and my aunt needed my mom. It was time to move.

Before then, I never really knew the true meaning of family. I only knew the simple version. The one that they teach you in Kindergarten, if not Pre-K. "Family is your mommy, your daddy, your sisters and your brothers," I would hear Mrs. Dickinson, my

59

Kindergarten teacher, say. But each year that I get older, I find how much more wrong she was. Family doesn't have to have a mom, a dad, sisters, or brothers. It just has to have people who care about one another so much that they would do anything for them. It could even contain people who are far from being related, but still experience the same feelings for one another that an average family does. After the move to Houston, when my family and I had settled into our new home, I finally got the whole meaning of the word "family". I had been receiving all of the pieces over the past few years, and I just needed one more, the true piece that completed "Family". By moving to Houston for my aunt, I finally received that piece, and the great puzzle of family finally made sense to me.

This is now my sixth year living in Houston. My aunt is remarried with two twin girls, Amelie and Ysabel, who turned four on February 20. It just goes to show that family, no matter what kind, does matter, and that even though you have these bad times, no matter how old you are, either six or sixty, you are always loved by someone. Always.

Mothers' Gifts

Jana Mullins

October 17, 1999. My forty-fifth birthday. This day marked not only my birth, but also my five-year anniversary as a Single Mother, a title I hadn't asked for, but one I was slowly growing accustomed to.

It was only five years before that I had gone through a life-changing divorce, bringing to a startling halt my twenty-year marriage and irrevocably changing my life and the lives of my three children. Suddenly, I was no longer the supportive wife, but instead a forty-year-old college student raising young children, starting a career and building a new life. I could not help but reflect on all the days I had felt so over-whelmed. At times, those five years seemed like an eternity. However, through the prayers, love and support of my family and friends, my little family of four not only survived, we began to thrive. I realized that in the midst of life's mending, my own life had gently and remarkably changed.

At work that morning, I found myself thinking about other single mothers, partic-ularly those who might have little support or encouragement. Knowing how hard it is to be a single mom, I picked up the phone and called Memorial Hermann Hospital, a Houston hospital that serves the uninsured. I asked for Labor and Delivery. Sandra, a kind,

soft-spoken woman answered the phone and I inquired if there had been a baby born that day. I explained that today was my birthday and I wanted to give a gift to a single mom, in particular one who might not have support around her. She said she would check and get back with me.

A few hours later I received a call, "I have a young single mother who has just had a baby boy. She is here alone." I told her I would be over that afternoon.

I was filled with a strange excitement and anticipation as I headed to the local grocery store. I eagerly purchased flowers, an iconic "It's A Boy Balloon" that I felt this new mother MUST have, a little stuffed teddy bear, a baby book and a card. In the card I placed a small monetary gift and explained that this gift was not for her newborn son, but something special just for her. In the note I congratulated her on the birth of her baby and on becoming the wonderful mother I knew she would be. I then brought my gift to the hospital and left it there to be delivered anonymously.

As I stepped outside those hospital doors

that afternoon, my eyes filled with tears and my heart felt complete. I stopped and offered a small prayer to God. I prayed this beautiful, young new family would forever feel God's love and support, and know that they were not alone in this world.

I haven't skipped a birthday at the hospital since.

This has become the highlight of my birthday and I cannot possibly imagine spending the day any other way. Over the years, I have received pictures of the moms and their babies. I have also received beautiful notes.

What they might not know, however, is that their notes and expressions of gratitude have always come to me, like small hugs, at moments when I needed them. In giving to other single mothers, my life has been enriched and I have over and over again abundantly received.

Ms. Pauline's Lap Robe

Karen Hahn

Come meet Ms. Pauline with me as I remember her. She's sitting in her recliner chair facing her front door, calling, "Come in. It's open." We go in.

There she is, grinning with her twinkling gray-blue eyes. Her short white hair is soft and thin on her round pink head. She's wearing a long polka-dotted jersey dress and gray tennis shoes. She looks small, tipped back in her worn recliner with her feet up and a cast below her arthritic knee. She waves us to her sofa. It's covered with a faded quilt and throw pillows. We make room and sit down.

Ms. Pauline apologizes for not getting up. "My ankle broke when I was standing in the kitchen last month. Osteoporosis. My bones are soft as soap, I guess. What can you expect at ninety-three? I'm supposed to stay off of it. I just have to give it time to heal. I've been using this walker over here to hobble around when I have to. I'm getting by all right." I see a big bag of yarn on the floor by the walker. On her lap is a pile of yarn with a crochet hook sticking out. Underneath is a multicolored lap robe in the making. I tell her, "I didn't know you like to crochet." She answers, "I don't. But the church had all of this yarn they were going to throw away. I told them not to waste it. I told them that

if someone brought it to me, I'd make lap robes for the people in the nursing home. I just kept thinking of those people you visit in the nursing home. I thought of how much they might like lap robes to keep them warm in their wheelchairs. This is my second one. It takes me a long time. But that's something I've got—a lot of time. I figured since I can't get out, I might as well do something to keep me occupied. And I keep thinking, at least I can still get around without a wheelchair."

Ms. Pauline gave me that lap robe. She said it was for someone in a wheelchair. But I still have it. I kept it. She died a few weeks after she finished it. I decided to put it in the sample Christmas gift basket we use every year to show what kinds of things to donate. Instead of giving the lap robe away, I made myself a promise to give Ms. Pauline's story away so her message would live on.

Her story is this.

Ms. Pauline's pastor had asked me to check on her every month or so because she was pretty much homebound and fighting depression. She could not get to church

63

anymore because it just plain wore her out to go anywhere. Her son had died the year before and she was still filled with grief at the sudden loss.

When our Coalition decided to make gift baskets for the homebound elderly, I put her on the list. A young student and I delivered one to her. When we came to her door with the basket full of goods and a teddy bear, Ms. Pauline was so moved that she made me tell her about all the things our Coalition was doing. She wrote everything down.

There was one thing she kept going back to and underlined over and over. That was this: "Collecting clothes and shoes for the children. Many children in this neighborhood do not have shoes or clothes for school or church. Many children go to bed hungry at night."

Ms. Pauline demanded that I take the basket back for the children. She picked up the phone while we were there and told her pastor that she wanted the church storeroom to be turned into a clothes and food pantry for the neighborhood. Then she sent us on our way because she said, "I have work to do."

One week later, Ms. Pauline called me, all excited. She asked me to go by her church. "My pastor has something to show you." I went. Pastor Terry showed me the storeroom. It was wall-to-wall clothing racks, filled with neatly hung clothes. The walls were lined with floor to ceiling metal shelves, stocked with canned food and bread goods. Amazed, I called her from the church. She said, "Now you tell those families to come to us. We don't want any children hungry. We don't want children ashamed to go to school or church.

"Tell them we will take care of them. Maybe I can't get out anymore, but I've been around the block a few times and everybody knows me around here. We'll keep that pantry stocked. You can't keep me out of ministry just because I can't get out!"

After she started this church pantry, Ms. Pauline's grief eased greatly. She kept the flow of donations going with her calls to family, friends, neighbors, and members. Her friend Ms. Virginia staffed the pantry before and after church events and ESL classes. Ms. Virginia called her every time and gave her a report on who came and what they still needed. Ms. Pauline tracked down those special needs. She had found a way to care for the next generation despite losing her only child.

Ms. Pauline's story is ours. We need to give to fully celebrate what we have. Sometimes what a person needs most is the opportunity to give.

Maybe you know a shut-in who might benefit from sending greeting cards for your group or a homebound member who might be delighted if someone asked her to call another shut-in for a friendly phone visit every day or a disabled person who would be grateful for a ride to a meeting so he could volunteer his expertise.

Look around you. Find someone who never gets asked to volunteer and ask that person to volunteer with you. Give the gift of service.

See this beautiful lap robe? My friend Ms. Pauline made it. She made it for all of us. Isn't it beautiful?

My Grandfather's Gift

Keiji Asakura

When I was a little boy my mother used to tell me not to ask or take gifts from others. She would tell me, "Be polite and say, no thank you."

Even when I was hungry or really thirsty, even sweet candies would temp me, I would say "No thank you. I am fine."

Her advice suited me fine until one day I received a call from my aunt that my grandfather's health was declining rapidly. I arranged my schedule and rushed to visit my grandfather. I rushed out the plane, through Customs to catch the last bullet train out of Tokyo to Niigata and with a few minutes of connecting time, I ran to catch the last local train to my grandfather's town, Nakajo. I was tired but I did not want to sleep, fearing that I would not wake up to get off the train at the station. Stepping out of the rail station, a hazy moon was above the mountain range east of the town. I remembered my hiking trip with my grandfather up in the mountains with tall Hinoki cypress trees.

Everyone was asleep when I finally arrived but my eldest aunt greeted me into the house.

Next morning, I found my grandfather lying in his bed at home. His doctor had sent him home, where he would feel more comfortable among his family. There was little the doctor could do at that point.

I sat down next to him, and he opened his eyes and greeted me. He already knew that I had arrived. He smiled and his voice was strong as always had been. He asked me how I was and how my work was, then he talked about flowers. Maybe my work, landscape architecture, had reminded him of flowers. He wanted flowers on our family shrine at the temple and at the family grave site. A religious man, my grandfather was well known at the town's Zen Buddhist temple. When we finished talking I went to buy some flowers. I went to the temple, spoke briefly to the priest and went into the family shrine hall. Rows and rows of family shrines, incense-filled air; I found our family shrine and placed a bouquet of flowers into a brass vase. I stepped outside to the family grave site inside the temple compound. I sat two bouquets there at the base of a large stone maker bearing our family name. I hurried back to the house with another bouquet. The bouquet was arranged and displayed where my grandfather could see. They were mostly chrysanthemums, yellow and white. My grandfather woke and saw the flowers, and I told him that flowers were also at the shine and the grave and described to him how the flowers were placed. He thanked me and commented how beautiful the flowers were. I was dismissive of his comment and said that it was really nothing I had done. Without thinking too much about his feelings, about how important this detail was at his last hours in his life, it was an all too familiar response that came from my mouth.

He had my aunt prepare money in an envelope and handed it to me. A shock! I said to him "No, I cannot take it." He told me to accept it. My aunt at his side looked at me. She was gesturing me to take it. I refused it all while my mother's voice from the past was echoing in my head. My grandfather thanked me again for the flowers and commented how far I had come to visit him.

My visit was short. I packed my suitcase and sat next to my grandfather to say goodbye. He was asleep and I looked at him for awhile. Tears came out of his closed eyes as I held his hands. His eyes still shut, he did not want to say goodbye.

He died the next morning after I left. I did not attend his funeral but asked my aunt for flowers at the shrine and at his grave.

I regret to this day that I could not receive his gift gracefully. It had meant so much to him for me to receive it. I have learned that in love of life there is an art of giving—and an art of receiving.

My House of Faith
Carolyn Watson

I could write my own book about how the generosity of others has enriched my life. Generosity directed towards me, my hometown of Houston and its parks, museums and cultural organizations, the educational institutions I've attended, the public radio and television stations that I enjoy. One recent experience is a favorite.

Since returning to Houston after completing my educational endeavors, I have wanted to live in The Heights, a historic neighborhood located near Downtown. I would routinely drive the streets, admire the late nineteenth- and early twentieth-century homes, pick out the ones I liked and the streets I favored most—and I would dream.

To take a step in realizing that dream, I purchased a one-bedroom condominium in the area and continued with my search. After about three years in the condo, the siren song of The Heights' bungalows kept calling me. My search for a house began.

I was clear about what I wanted: house in original condition (some Heights homes have creative—but not up-to-code or attractive—additions or modifications), preferably an original- or near-original-owner house (those that have been rented out have lots of wear and tear) and a garage. And it needed to be within my price range!

I focused my search on Woodland Heights, a subdivision within the Greater Heights community that has a commitment to historic preservation, beautiful oak trees and hosts the annual Christmas celebration, "Lights in the Heights." My weekends were spent driving the streets, noting "For Sale" signs and then calling to obtain sales prices.

Prices were higher than I had anticipated. Even a fixer-upper was out of reach. My dad suggested I purchase a vacant lot and then build on it. We even spent a day driving the neighborhood, noting vacant lots. After going through all kinds of permutations with the numbers (lot cost + construction price, etc.), I realized that wasn't a workable plan either. It is now eight months later.

Disappointed, tired and out of ideas, one night I prayed and placed my desire in God's hands, and told Him if He wanted me to have a house in The Heights, then I was trusting Him to make it happen. If not, then there was another place I was supposed to be.

AS I REFLECT ON THAT TIME OF MY LIFE, I AM OVERWHELMED WITH GRATITUDE TO GOD, NOT ONLY FOR MY HOUSE...

...BUT ALSO FOR SENDING ME GENEROUS AND SUPPORTIVE FRIENDS AND FAMILY WHO TOOK THE TIME AND CARE TO HELP MAKE MY DREAM A REALITY.

the electrical system and the addition of new siding. I served as general contractor and hired the plumber, electrician, roofer, house leveler, carpenter, sheet rocker, AC installer and painter. The process took nearly a year, because I was working fulltime and took my time in selecting subcontractors. My dad provided a lot of elbow grease and know-how during the process.

During that time, some friends and I had arranged a co-op, whereby we would take turns on Saturdays each quarter to work on each other's homes. Each Saturday workday was akin to a blitzkrieg, with eight of us engrossed in various tasks, with the goal of completing our work by sundown or earlier. On my particular day, great progress was made in painting, removing the AC window units that seemed to have melded into the window frames, landscaping and more.

Many other friends came forward, asking to help. Working side by side with my friends made many evenings less lonely and the house project less daunting. Marla, a dear friend from elementary school, was there from beginning to end and her support was invaluable. All these helpers shared in my joy and I had a taste of what an Amish barn-raising might feel like.

At different points in the project, I did become weary and frustrated, asking myself why I thought it was a good idea to buy a fixer-upper and swearing to myself that I would never, ever fix up a house again. Never. Ever.

At month thirteen after purchase, I was out of patience. I asked God for some help

After that prayer, I had a realization that though Woodland Heights was out of reach at that time, perhaps I needed an interim step. I decided to be open to other parts of The Heights, to purchasing there and, down the road, moving to Woodland Heights.

The next morning I called my realtor. I told him I was going to expand my horizons and look outside Woodland Heights. He told me he saw a house that morning on a listing tour that I would like. It was for sale at a reasonable price and met my criteria. "How exciting," I replied, "I'll see you tonight after work for a tour." Dead silence on the other end of the line. Then I clued into why he was quiet. "I need to come now, right?" I literally walked out the door that moment with my purse and within two hours had drawn up an offer and a contract.

The purchase process transpired like a dream, and the purchase closed on schedule.

Then the real work began. I decided to move in with my parents during the reno-vation process. The house was truly in its 1929 condition, save for a few updates to

to finish the house so I could move in. The next day, my friend Debbie asked when I was going to move into my house. I told her that I was still working on it. Debbie exclaimed, "We need a Habitat for Carolyn Day!" referring to the Habitat for Humanity program. She instructed me to make a list of the tasks I needed completed and offered to organize the workers and get our supplies.

Around three weeks later, I had a cadre of my colleagues in philanthropy working at my house. Debbie crawled up in the attic with me, clearing out seventy years of junk. Esther and Jana did everything from screw in switch plates to clean the bathtub. Nancy and husband, Tex, planted grass, plants and flowers around the perimeter of my house. Mom and dad installed my window coverings. My house was ready for move in.

As I reflect on that time of my life, I am overwhelmed with gratitude to God, not only for my house but also for sending me generous and supportive friends and family who took the time and care to help make my dream a reality. The experience showed me that once I stopped striving to accomplish my goal alone—by placing my dreams in God's hands—I would reap gifts I never could imagine.

My home in The Heights is now much more than a shelter for me. It is a symbol of faith realized. And daily, as I move from room to room, I am blessed by my remembrances of the people who helped me along the way. My home is a living lesson in love—and in life.

My Own Needs First

Gwen Dittmar

I am slowly finding the more I live my life from the state of loving, I experience loving in all acts, giving, receiving, being, without willing or trying. This was challenging for me in the past, for most of my life. I felt selfish or unworthy of taking care of my own needs and emotions first.

Quite frankly, I did not even know what my needs and emotions were, or how to take care of them, because I had repressed them for so long, put them aside to deal with at another time, or prioritized the needs and emotions of others in my life before my own.

I think the most amazing gift I have received is giving myself back to me. The love and respect and joy I now feel inside are unlike any gift, present, or act I could provide for another or give another. I know that the love that I feel inside vibrates into my world, my work, my family, my friends, my enthusiasms. The more I take care of my own needs, the more I allow others to empower themselves and take care of their own needs.

"COMPASSION FOR OTHERS BEGINS WITH KINDNESS TO OURSELVES."

PEMA CHODRON

71

Nature vs. Nurture

Marie Davis

For nineteen years I wrapped myself up in the lives of my children. I was concentrating on holding onto a family unity I worked so hard to achieve. I had faith in the ties of love that bound us. The question of nature vs. nurture was one to which I had an easy answer.

I was convinced environment and shared experiences were way more important than genetics. I knew I could be "everything" to my adopted children. If I was a loving, nurturing parent there would be no need for them to know anything else. I shared with them all the background information I was given by the agency. Surely there would be no need to meet the person who gave them life. I never imagined meeting their birthparents the day they were placed in my arms. I was certain, as I was told, that my children's birthparents had forgotten and gone on with their lives putting these children behind them. I never gave much thought to the life of their birth parents. Even though I was thankful for the depth of their sacrifices, I didn't have a sense of a "real" person.

There were lots of uncertainties when that first letter arrived from my son's birthmother. I did not want to "share" my precious son. Meeting her would surely jeopardize our hard-earned family stability. She crossed a sacred line in contacting us and was "invading" our lives. Would I be closed out of part of my closeness to my son? How would their reconnection impact my parenting role? How would or could she fit in to our family? I had put in all the hard work and effort for nineteen years. Would she now replace me? My emotions swung from confident to intense panic. I wanted to lock my doors and have her to ride off into the sunset. The only problem was...she wouldn't go!

Opening my heart to my son's birthmother, Karen, would be the hardest thing I would ever do in my life. Part of parenting is putting a child's need first. She did this at the beginning of his life and I had to do it now. I had to put lots of fears and insecurities aside and be able to find room in my heart for what I thought was an impossibility.

The anticipation of meeting Karen was far worse than the actual meeting. With a little bit of risk and a huge amount of faith, hope and love, we met during the summer of 2003. Meeting Karen has been a huge and wonder-

72

fully overwhelming experience for me. I have a deep, humble feeling of gratitude to her. There have been lots of tears as I've recalled the most important thing that ever happened in my life. She gave me the chance of being the mom I longed to be. I now could see the "real" person of Karen with her anguish and extraordinary pain in her heart that was not to go away until she could meet her birth son for the second time and fill it up with the love of that boy. I came to see a courageous young lady who did indeed relinquish her rights, but not her love and concern for John. Our relationship has evolved slowly over time by sharing our lives, loves, beliefs, values, and a deep level of connection with our shared love of John. Each step along the way I have gained confidence in myself and trust in her. For me, sharing the memories, love, and joy of raising my son with the person who gave me that chance has been comforting and validating. For Karen it has been a slow healing of her sorrow and a peacefulness to now know of his favorite color, his dog's name, his love of cars, and his dislike of fruitcakes. For both of us, there has been gratitude all around.

The successful reunion solidifies in my mind and heart that it was the right thing to do, though the hardest thing I have ever anticipated doing in my life. I am happy to have been able to open my heart to Karen. I now can't imagine not knowing her. I am pleased to have been able to honor my son by blessing his reunion. I am thankful Karen gave my son the gift of life and now the gift of blessing me as his mom. Our intriguing relationship has turned into more than a friendship or even a sisterhood. Loving her has been a natural extension of loving John. The more I see Karen's features and qualities,

the more my love extends to her as part of him. Most importantly, Karen has added a dimension to my son's life for which I am forever grateful. John has a confidence and stronger sense of who he is. It was good for him to learn of his heritage. He now knows where he gets his hazel eyes and his slim frame. He shares her love of the outdoors. He knows where he came from. He feels a little bit stronger and knows he "belongs."

Compassion and kindness of heart by two families has made this all work. Two aspects of John 's life, nature and nurture, have been joined together. Each visit of the two families builds more concrete connections to one another. We have succeeded in blending together in a unique way as an extended family dedicated to John. He has the special love of two families who truly care about one another and want him to have the best life possible. I have an easy answer now to the question of nature vs. nurture. They are equally important.

One Mentor Made a Difference

Carole Little

When I was in the fifth grade, I was chosen to partake in a mentoring program with three other children. Our mentors were a young married couple who were graduate students. They took me on my very first trip to the city library, which was the most magnificent building I had ever seen.

Just imagine, all those books were free to use! No strings attached. From that day forward, I went to the public library as often as I could, whenever I could, and I always borrowed the maximum number of books. My escape was through reading. It took me to such wonderful places.

On another occasion, the young couple invited our group to their tiny apartment for dinner. We all took part in preparing the meal and to this day, I remember stirring the spaghetti and chatting in the kitchen. Our hostess asked me if I had given any thought to going to college. I told her that our family would never have enough money for that. She and her husband then talked about how to get free money for college. They explained that they were graduate students and they had received scholarship money, partially based on need and partially based on academics. From that day forward, I knew I would someday go to college.

I ended my senior year in a foster home

by choice and won a full scholarship to Boston University. It was the greatest achievement in my young life! In my junior year, an injury sustained earlier in the year resulted in a full month of hospitalization. Although I made up all the coursework for the first semester, one of my professors decided that even though I got an A- in her course, I couldn't have fully benefited from it since I had missed more than three classes. The academic review board (of which she was a member and had a vote) agreed with her by a vote of three to two. The Dean called me in right before final exams at the end of second semester to inform me that I would have to repeat first semester before continuing. Therefore, I would not receive credit for the second semester courses that were contingent upon her first semester course. My scholarship would not cover the extra courses and living expenses needed for me to repeat a whole year.

My dream was shattered and I walked

around in a daze until reality set in and I had to get a job quick or be evicted. Thus, I entered the working world in Boston with no college degree, a long list of work-study and summer jobs and a high school diploma.

My professional career began in 1978 with a job as a mental health aide at the Walter E. Fernald School in Waltham, MA. I wanted to make a difference in the world. I had worked my way up to the position of "Mental Health Supervisor" in a facility that cared for severely retarded adolescents. It did not take long to figure out the system betrayed the very clients it swore to protect and care for. I felt powerless against state bureaucracy and the union to make the necessary changes. I vowed that some day I would be in a position to make the tough decisions, but at that point the system won out. I decided to sell all my earthly possessions and do something more with my life. After many years of working overseas and then in health and human services, I entered the world of nonprofit management in the summer of 1998, when I was given the opportunity to serve as the leader of a ministry in Houston whose primary goal was to serve those in crisis. A few weeks after my arrival, I began

to realize I had finally found my niche. The sum of my life's experiences had led me to that wonderful place. I could empathize with individuals in need as well as with my employees and volunteers who experienced the ups and downs of daily life.

My personal mantra was always to live a purpose-driven life. Initially I thought if I could make a difference in just one person's life, my own life would have meaning. I never dreamed that I would have the opportunity to serve in a greater capacity. So you see, I owe it to my fifth grade mentor to finish.

I never dreamed that I would have the opportunity to serve in a greater capacity. So you see, I owe it to my fifth grade mentor to finish what I started back in 1976. Thirty years later, in January of 2006, I enrolled in college as a full time student, mom, and wife, with a full time job. I graduated with my degree at the same time my first born 75 entered college. Presently, I am pursuing a Master's in Coaching in order to assist others reach their full potential. Mentoring is truly a life changing experience. One person's caring made all the difference in my life. My mentor saw the potential in me.

One Vote of Confidence

Twila Ross

I was born and raised in Mobile, Alabama. I came from a family of hard-working people but not people who had the desire or opportunity for education. When I was thirteen, a preacher's wife asked me where I was intending to go to college.

I laughed as I told her I had no intention of going to college. The idea was at that time inconceivable. No one in my family had graduated from high school much less gone to college. She looked at me and said, "Of course you are going to college. You are much too smart not to go to college."

In the weeks that followed that comment, she made arrangements for me to travel with the high school class to visit a small church college in Tennessee. I was so drawn to this college and to the idea that I just might be able to go to college. I took a picture of the college administrative building and tacked it on my wall in my bedroom. You might imagine the teasing and ridicule that followed. Five years later I, by simply putting one foot in front of the other, and with the courage that only God could give me, completed my application and was accepted to this little college.

In the fall of that year, I left my home and never returned except for visits. I spent my summers doing missionary work in different states and countries. The in-between details are not that necessary, but the main point of my story is one woman believed that there was more possible for me than I had dared to imagine.

For the last forty years, I have worked in the field of social services as a caseworker, therapist, executive director, and consultant. My life has touch thousands of individuals, including a staff member for whom I was responsible. My focus has always been helping disadvantaged individuals and helping people navigate complicated systems to gain some power and presence in their lives. My passion for people is my life. I have loved my jobs and have never really worked a day in my life.

Now, this fall my daughter will graduate from college. Her major? Social work, of course. And the kindness goes on and on. All this from a simple sentence and a vote of confidence. A vote of confidence for which I will always be grateful. A simple vote of confidence that changed my life. How can I offer less?

"Spread love everywhere you go:
First of all in your own house.
Give love to your children, to your wife
or husband,to a next door neighbor…
Let no one come to you
without leaving better or happier.
Be the living expression of God's kindness;
kindness in your face,
kindness in your eyes,
kindness in your smile
and kindness in your warm greeting."

MOTHER TERESA

*"There never was a person
who did anything worth doing,
who did not receive more than he gave."*

HENRY WARD BEECHER

Paulina Cerilla, Giver of Dignity

Sam Burkett, Grade 6

I am a dancer and she is a singer; we are completely different. She is Paulina Cerilla, the kindest person in the world. I started Musical Theater last year at Theater Under the Stars, and Paulina started at the exact same time.

We were in a summer camp there working on a review for some of the teachers who worked there. We auditioned for the same solo in a singing number. We both made it and then our friendship sparked like a blow torch. We talked and said how good we each were at singing and dancing and how we had such a fun time working on this duet, which was ironically about friendship.

When the three weeks ended it was so depressing and sad for the both of us. After a few days, I couldn't stand not being with her and laughing until we cried. But then one day my mom called me telling me that we had both gotten a callback for an audition together. It wasn't the same role because I'm a boy and she's a girl, but it was in the same ensemble. I was ecstatic and couldn't wait too see her again. When we both were at the audition, we talked and laughed for hours. But then I was supposed to go up into the room and sing a song. I was freaking out, but then Paulina rushed to my aid and gave me the most moving speech on how I could do this, and how the directors wanted me to be the one, and be the best for them so they could have an easy choice.

That was the first time I felt I had true confidence in myself and that I could do it. I walked into that audition room and nailed it. Ten minutes later I learned that I had gotten the role. I was so proud of myself that I ran around the room screaming, so excited. Paulina then gave me the "I told you so" talk about how she knew I could do it. I didn't care and was so happy that she had been there and told me the way to have dignity and hold my head up high. Because of Paulina Cerilla I have Dignity.

Sharing a Nanny

Rev. Gerald J. DeSobe, Ph.D.

It was a sad and frightening time. My spouse had died four months after the birth of my son.

I was in my early thirties, one year removed from having received my Ph.D. and trying to prove to myself and establish to my colleagues that I was a competent pastoral counselor and psychologist.

I was a now single parent who had basically no child-rearing experience or expertise and was trying to figure out how to keep my life together personally and professionally, during this difficult period where my son needed both my emotional investment and financial income.

A major concern of mine was child care. Who would take care of my son in a good way while I was at work? The hospital for which I worked had a child-care center but it was notorious for having the many children there pass one disease after another from child to child. How could I take care of my son and my patients at the same time if I had to be home often with a sick child? Other child-care options were no better.

Into this emotional maelstrom angels appeared. A physician couple with whom I worked at the hospital had also recently had their first child. After his birth, they had hired a woman to take care of the child at their home throughout the day. Knowing of my situation, they offered to have their nanny take care of my son during the day as well. To share their nanny was not in their original plan. In fact they looked forward to their son receiving individual attention and care. Yet, they saw my need and offered their help to me immediately and without reservation.

For over a year my son and their son shared a nanny. Our cooperation worked very well. Both boys received the care and attention they needed and I had the comfort of knowing my son was well cared for as I went about caring for people who came to me for help. What a relief and support to me not only professionally, but emotionally, as I lived out the single parent role and tried to develop competent child care skills.

My son is now a man. He survived my awkward early parenting! Both he and I were blessed when I married a woman who has been a loving wife and wonderful mother. But, I still believe today that the gift given by two caring physicians of a safe place for my son to be made a significant difference in my son's and my life. For that gift I will be always grateful.

Sliver of Hope

Jay McMahan

When I was sixteen, I had been diagnosed with a severe form of muscular dystrophy. This original diagnosis was grim, with a generous estimate of three to five years remaining in my too-short life.

The predicted muscle deterioration and looming limitations were quite opposite of how I had lived my life to date as a young, athletic and creative person full of dreams. With this prognosis, I felt these dreams were taken away from me as if they had never existed!

The doctors had suggested using physical therapy to slow down the inevitable deterioration. However, God provided me with a heavy dose of faith that allowed me to envision a possible way out. I saw the therapy as rehabilitation, as a route to returning to my normal life.

When I started the physical therapy sessions, I related my hopes and ideas to my therapist, Dan. Up to this point, every doctor and medical staff member would offer a smile of pity whenever I brought up my dreams of rehabilitation. However, Dan listened patiently and proceeded to map out a course of action with me.

During the next twelve months, Dan patiently detailed my progress, analyzed my setbacks and measured my successes. He was able to convert the structured training I had used as an athlete into a motivational tool to keep me on track. Within a few months, we had proven that this course of action led to great progress, which was contradictory to the doctors' original prognosis. This hard-won progress resulted in a new round of tests and, more importantly, the removal of the stigma of limitations surrounding my disease. Although more questions than answers remain about muscular dystrophy (and still no cure to be found), I am alive and kicking and focused on what I am able to do rather than allowing my disability to dictate what type of life I lead.

Dan's belief in me offered a sliver of hope that was permanently embedded in my psyche. This relationship and experience proved that even though a task may seem impossible or unrealistic, sometimes the best thing you can do for a person is to simply support them and allow fate to take the reigns.

Heart, Hope and a Little Beshert

Amelia Ribnick Kleiman

"Beshert" is understood to be the precept that all that occurs
in every aspect of our lives is orchestrated by a Divine hand....

My husband Eric and I both wanted kids. Some might argue just how many, but we always knew, more than one. So, when it took us seven years and 4 miscarriages to have our first child, Brett, in 1996, we knew we would not have an easy time having a second child. Little did we know then just how hard it would be.

After several unsuccessful surgeries, Eric and I decided to adopt. In March 2002, after looking at our options, we decided to adopt internationally. After numerous fits and starts with the Russian adoption process, we were a little gun shy, feeling anxious every time the phone rang or we received an email from our adoption agency. In February 2003, we got word about a 5-month-old little girl from the Vladivostok region in far eastern Russia. She was so cute, with big blue eyes, but we worried: what if? what if a Russian family takes her? what if the medical reports aren't good? what if someone ransoms our papers? All things that had already happened to us. But, never without hope or the feeling that "our baby" must be out there some-where, we had the medicals and video reviewed. All came back good. On February 18, 2003, we accepted the referral for our first daughter.

Russian law normally requires two trips on international adoptions. On the first, you meet the child, get interviewed by the Russian authorities, and finish the necessary paperwork. These trips are short, typically lasting about 8 days. The second trip, about 4–5 weeks later, lasts a little longer, and usually ends with parents bringing home their newly adopted child or children.

We left Houston two weeks after our acceptance to head to Russia to meet our new daughter. We scrambled to get clothes for the Siberian winter, and we wanted to take as much as we could for our baby and the orphanage.

Flying across the Pacific by way of San Francisco, and through South Korea, then into Russia, it all seemed so surreal. But, as we flew into the heart of Siberia, it all became reality. We were actually landing in Russia, about to meet our new daughter.

Driving to the orphanage, it felt as if we had driven into "the old country." Blanketed in frozen snow, many of the homes and villages along the partially completed "major highway" between Vladivostok and Ussuriysk looked like the village from "Fiddler on the Roof".

At the orphanage, it felt like we were in another movie, only this time, sadly, it was "Oliver Twist". There were attempts to make the place look presentable to us and other foreigners, but a closer inspection revealed peeling paint, cracked walls, poorly ventilated rooms, drafty windows, and little kids dressed in two or three layers of clothing to keep them warm in the middle of March's still bitter cold.

All of this soon became unimportant. After preliminary introductions and a brief discussion, all in Russian, one of the workers brought in a tightly-wrapped baby and thrust it into my arms, along with a baby-bottle of sorts. I had no idea what the lady was saying, even though our translator was right there, as I had been transported into another world. Our beautiful daughter was now in my arms, a living, breathing child, who would be a part of us forever.

She had searing, deep blue eyes, the kind that look right through you, and the sweetest smile I had ever seen. Despite the language barrier, and the odd baby bottle, I understood that she was to be fed. My mother's instincts took over, and soon, our daughter was nursing in my arms. After a good burp, she fell asleep on my shoulder, and stayed there for another hour.

After she woke up, Eric finally got to hold her. I took one look at her lying there with Eric, and said "She's definitely a Jenna". Jenna looked so little in Eric's arms as he serenaded her, and for a 5 month-old, she was, weighing only about 8 pounds. She held tight to his fingers, staring up into the only male face she probably had ever seen this close-up.

The next few days were a blur, as we endured the 2 hour drive each way on the bumpy highway, morning and night, to spend every possible waking moment at the orphanage with our daughter. At that point, Jenna was our daughter, even though the Russian court hadn't said so. In fact, as far as we were concerned, as soon as we had said "Yes" back on February 18th, this beautiful little girl was ours! Our task was to bond with her, to hold her, to love her, and to let her know that she would soon be part of a caring family, with a big brother, three grandmas, a grandpa, aunts, uncles, cousins, and friends...all waiting to welcome her.

Jenna appeared healthy. But, like all of the kids in the drafty orphanage, she seemed to have a little cold. As recommended, we had brought a medicine chest of remedies from home, which we gave to the Orphanage head. We also bought other stronger medicines once we got there for her rash and her cold as medicine is something most of the orphanages can't afford. During our visits Jenna seemed to be getting better, but when it was time to say goodbye, I was so upset.

The orphanage director tried to re-assure us that they would take care of our daughter, but I was not handling this well, and I did not have a good feeling. I wished it were already our next trip and that we were taking her home, not leaving her with strangers in a strange cold land, 10,000 miles away. The flight home was awful and wonderful at the same time. I felt pain and angst at having left our little girl, but I couldn't wait to get home and share our impending joy with everyone!

When we got home, the videos of our visits with Jenna were so cute. There was one where we got her laughing and giggling, and our family and friends fell in love with our baby girl, just as we had. We couldn't wait to bring her home to all this love, and we prayed that things would go well.

But, due to delays, the normal time between trips stretched into nearly 9 weeks. When we finally got our travel date, we all breathed a sigh of relief. We were almost there. Our prayers were about to come true, and soon, our baby, Jenna, would be home with us.

Three nights before we were to leave, we learned that Jenna was sick in a Russian hospital, with acute bronchitis. We frantically starting emailing our agency liaison, but could not get more information other than that she was in a children's hospital and would probably be kept there until we arrived, since the orphanage was understaffed and the hospital could take better care of her. Never having encountered the Russian hospital system, we pictured a children's hospital like Texas Children's Hospital in Houston, with clean rooms, highly-trained staff, and plenty of equipment and medicine to take care of a little baby with bronchitis. We offered to send money ahead to pay for medicine, but were told that wasn't necessary. Prayers were all we had to give now. They kept trying to re-assure us, but I was so anxious.

Flying from Hawaii to Seoul and then on to Vladivostok, I was so excited: our dreams and prayers were getting so much closer. Yet,

that nagging feeling stayed with me. I kept telling myself that Jenna was in good hands, that the orphanage director had promised to take care of her, but still....

When we encountered problems in customs, my concerns only heightened. After finally escaping the gauntlet of Russian customs hell, we went out to find our hosts. We were told that Jenna had been moved to ICU at another children's hospital, and we would be going straight there.

To say that we did not find the kind of ICU or children's hospital we expected would be a laughable understatement. We had stepped back into pre-war Russia. The equipment, furnishings, and treatments were all from 60 years before. The hospital even had a cow grazing on the front lawn.

But we weren't worried; we just wanted to see and hold our daughter, and let her know that we were there, and she was safe. Seeing Jenna was heart wrenching. She had been small before, but after almost two months in the hospital she was so little and frail. I could not hold in the tears.

We spoke to her softly, and let her know how much we loved her, and she seemed to respond. In fact, the nurses said, through our translator, hearing our voices was the first time she had perked up in days. When we were allowed to hold her, it was such an unbelievable feeling. She was asleep at first, and when she opened her eyes, they seemed to speak to us: "I've been waiting for you, where have you all been?" Every time Eric spoke she followed him with her searing blue eyes, but soon, she became tired, and we had to put her down to rest.

I will not go into detail of the days that followed—the attempts to move her closer to us, to a bigger hospital with more experienced doctors and more modern equipment; the all night calls to our doctors in Houston at TCH; the insurance issues trying to get her airlifted at first to anywhere but there, like Japan; and later, the attempts to airlift her home; the fights over her care with the Russian doctors; the medicines we had to buy; the trip to have a passport picture taken of Jenna, tubes and all; the two hour trips daily each way to and from the hospital—all of this while moving ahead with the adoption process back in Vladivostok

OUR TASK WAS TO BOND WITH HER, TO HOLD HER, TO LOVE HER, AND TO LET HER KNOW THAT SHE WOULD SOON BE PART OF A CARING FAMILY, WITH A BIG BROTHER, THREE GRANDMAS, A GRANDPA, AUNTS, UNCLES, COUSINS, AND FRIENDS... ALL WAITING TO WELCOME HER.

When our court hearing on the adoption finally arrived on May 15, 2003, it was beyond surreal. The Russian prosecutor, in full Russian military uniform, grilled us in Russian about what kind of parents we would be, why we wanted this child, and what we would tell her about Russia when she was older, all overseen by the stern countenance of the presiding female Russian judge. All we could think of was, please God, let this be final so we can get Jenna out of here and take her home where she will have a chance at a better life. Finally, amidst a jumble of Russian, it was done and legal. Jenna was officially our daughter, and we, her parents.

Now that she was ours and not a ward of the state, things changed, for the good and bad. We were completely responsible for decisions about her, but the state was still in charge of her care. Until we got all the papers back from Moscow, we could not leave the country with her.

In the interim, we continued to work on airlifting her out. The costs would be exorbitant, and insurance would not cover it all, but we are blessed to be from one of the most caring communities in the world. Calls flew back and forth to Houston, France, Israel, London, New Jersey, and what seemed like all points in between. Our community— friends, family and even acquaintances—were pulling together to help raise money for us to get Jenna out. From 10,000 miles away, they told us not to let money stop us: "Just get her home".

So, that was what we were determined to do. Saturday before the medivac plane was to arrive in Russia on Monday to take us home, I was on the phone with the flight nurse discussing some of the trip details. Jenna's condition had gone up and down for the ten days since her adoption was final, but the night before we had a call that she was stable. We just prayed that she could hold on for 2 more days.

Then, there was a knock at our hotel room door. The minute I opened it, I knew. The faces of our translator and agency liaison told it all. Jenna was gone. I stood in disbelief as they told me our baby—our little angel—was gone. How could this be? Just 8 hours before, Jenna was stable, and we were making plans to take her home.

The next few days were a blur. Getting approval to bring Jenna home to bury her in our family plot proved difficult due to the SARS epidemic, which was occurring just across the border in China. But, after endless red tape, we were finally in the Vladivostok airport, waiting for the flight to take us home with Jenna.

85

Eric and I had already starting discussing that when our grieving was over, we would come back and adopt another baby. But as we stood in tears, watching our daughter's casket being loaded onto the plane, it was the furthest thing from our minds. So, when our agency liaison asked if we would be interested in going to meet another little girl—a 13 month old who they said looked just like me—it was difficult to handle. She was in an orphanage not far from the airport. If we met her now, we would only have to make one trip if we wanted to adopt her.

We were stunned. Our daughter Jenna, our baby girl, was in a casket. We were going home to bury her. How could we think past that? The agency was just trying to comfort us in the best way they knew, and trying to save another Russian child.

As we returned home, friends and family took over to make sure we were okay. Jenna's funeral, held just 2 weeks after her adoption was final, was a wonderful tribute to her, and to our family and friends and to the community who had supported us throughout the whole ordeal. Jenna was laid to rest next to her grandfather, for whom she had been named. She would forever have a family to love and remember her.

At the funeral, Eric spoke beautifully of the impact that Jenna's life would have on so many others, and our wish that she be remembered as a beacon of hope for all children in need of homes and families. He also expressed our commitment that this would not be the end of the story. We would go back to Russia and bring home another child to complete our family.

Before we could think of going back, we needed time to grieve. We also needed financial help to make another adoption

possible. We had depleted most of our savings for the fertility treatments and Jenna's adoption. With the extra costs of Jenna's illness, our extended stay in Russia, long distance calls home, and funeral costs, there were hardly any funds left for us to complete our mission. We had gotten some money back from the agency, but not nearly enough to start again. We knew we could not make this happen alone. It was time to put pride aside and be open to the help others were offering us. Once again, friends and family, and the community came to our rescue, raising the money that would allow us to move forward again.

Jenna will always be our first daughter. She is always with us, each and every day. But we knew, at some point, another baby was out there, waiting. So, we started all over again—more paperwork, with more restrictions this time, another home-study, and more stress. In mid-July we received a call about a 15 month-old girl, and somehow, the stress all faded. When we discovered the referral was the little girl they had told us about at the airport, we were dumb-founded. They explained they had held her for us. Diana, the agency director, told us that her name was Nadezhda, but that her nickname was Nadia, which meant "hope" in Russian.

Eric and I were both on the phone and almost simultaneously we said, "It's beshert." The agency head, a former Jewish refusnik from Russia, knew the word, but she asked, "What do you mean?" We explained that once we had decided to go back for another child, we had begun to talk about names. We had settled on "Hope", since that was what we had, and that was what we wanted to give to our child. At that moment, on the phone with Diana, we knew and understood all that had come before. Jenna, our beautiful angel, had come into our lives to open our hearts and the hearts of all of those around us. She was God's messenger, and she was meant to be the one to lead us to our hope for the future.

We returned to Russia in the fall of that year. We stayed at the same hotel we had stayed during our first two trips. We met the young Jewish man who had sat with Jenna's body in the morgue in Vladivostok. His mother was the leader of the newly re-born Jewish community in Vlad. We broke bread with the new Rabbi there, that community's first rabbi since before World War II. We joined their small community to celebrate Yom Kippur, and we cried as we celebrated Jenna's first birthday on October 7, 2003. Two days later, on October 9, 2003, Jacklyn's adoption was final. She had just turned 18 months old.

Jacklyn arrived in Houston to join her new family on October 18th, 2003, almost 18 months to the day after we first started our adoption paperwork. In Judaism, the number "18" is special. It signifies "chai", which means life. When we looked at all the "signs", we felt that this was meant to be—that Jacklyn truly was our beshert.

After Jenna died, we had set up a memorial fund in her name that will eventually help doctors from Texas Children's Hospital and Baylor College of Medicine train and support pediatric medical professionals who care for orphans and other children in the former Soviet Union. It was our small tribute to her, our way of giving back, and something we hoped would someday help make sure other children could be spared Jenna's fate.

Recently, I went to work for Baylor College of Medicine, the teaching arm of Texas Children's Hospital, whose doctors helped us at so many turns with Jenna and Jacklyn, and where Jacklyn is now taking therapy for a neurological disorder from her days in the orphanage. When I was asked during my interview why I wanted to work at Baylor College of Medecine, I explained what happened to Jenna and said that I couldn't imagine a better place for me to be to help the doctors who helped us with Jenna and Jacklyn. It was beshert that I was to be at Baylor College of Medecine to bring our story full circle, as it was now my turn to give back just some of the love and support that we received.

Even today, we know that we would not have Jacklyn had we not lost Jenna. But more importantly, we know that we would not have been able to bring Jenna to her final resting place with her forever family or go back and adopt Jacklyn had it not been for the community that pulled together and gave us so much, both emotionally and financially.

To this day, we have no idea who contributed to the fund for Jenna's expenses and Jacklyn's adoption. But every now and then, when we are out with Jacklyn, someone will come up and say "Is this Jacklyn—our 'community' baby? Look how big she has grown!" and we know!

When she is old enough to understand, we will tell Jacklyn how lucky she is to be part of such a special community, one that gave of their hearts to two little girls, girls who had no family, and now, have a whole community that calls them their own.

87

The Gift Worth Waiting For

Victoria DePaul

Today is one of those days that I will carry in my memory. We all have days such as this one. These are the days that cause us to stop, take a deep breath, reflect.

The events of days such as these cause us to examine our priorities. Today is such a day, you see, for today I was told that Ms. Joyce is dying.

I think of Ms. Joyce as my second Mom, a spiritual Mom of sorts. We share a special bond of friendship and camaraderie and yet it is so much more than that. Ms. Joyce is a brilliant woman. In her eighty-three years of life, she has maintained a keen interest in literature, history, the arts, philosophy and current events; we never lack topics for conversation.

I met Ms. Joyce through my friendship with her daughter Veronica. The family was assembling because of the sudden, unexpected death of Veronica's daughter. The first time we met, I felt as though I was entertaining royalty (and of course now I know I was, because hers is a true regal spirit). Ms. Joyce and other members of the family arrived at Veronica's home earlier than anticipated. Veronica was not available, so I stepped up to the plate and assumed my role as friend, neighbor and hostess.

Since the family hails from the United Kingdom, I made an immediate offer of tea, which was graciously accepted. I scurried for mugs and teabags and placed them in the microwave. As I turned around with the awkwardness that accompanies all encounters with new persons, particularly one where grief is present, I was met with horrified stares. Ms. Joyce, eyes wide said, "Surely you will not be serving tea from mugs in a microwave. Where is the teapot? Veronica must have a teapot!" A teapot. Those were really for tea? In my house, and I suspect many other American households, teapots were for decorating shelves, storing pennies, dust collectors.

The four of us, Ms. Joyce, two of her daughters and me, searched cabinets and shelves and eventually uncovered a teapot. I stared at the pot wondering how I was supposed to make tea with this. Being creative and wanting to please, I filled it with water, placed twenty teabags inside with the tags ever so neatly lined on the edges, replaced the cover as best as I could and placed the pot in the microwave. The looks of horror had not diminished but by now we had all come to the silent conclusion that if we were going to get anywhere near a cup of tea on this day, resignation was the best option.

As the tea continued to brew in the microwave, Ms. Joyce asked, "Do you know where Veronica keeps the cozy?" A cozy—no chance I could fake this one. She returned to the cupboard where the teapot was found and pulled out a cozy and handed it to me. It was the strangest pot holder I had ever seen and quite awkward to use. My hand just didn't fit, but I appreciated that she was concerned that I might burn myself when I removed the teapot from the microwave. She watched, obviously amused, as I clumsily poured the tea into mugs. As she accepted the tea she said with a smile, "Tea from bags in a teapot in a microwave. How interesting." Does tea come from someplace other than a teabag? I made a mental note to investigate that at some future point.

Such was our introduction. Over the next months and years our paths crossed many times and often overlapped. In the past three years, the family has had five deaths and two sisters with cancer. Throughout these trying times Ms. Joyce and I became quite close. Veronica and another daughter, Karen, were both diagnosed with cancer at the same time. Ms. Joyce struggled in her advanced years to care for them both. I provided as much assistance as I could to lighten the load. It was during these months that our relationship blossomed. She called me her fifth daughter, a position I cherished.

We spent hours discussing current world events and politics. Ms. Joyce lived in London during WWII and offered a personal per- spective of history that I could never have obtained from a text. We also debated for many an hour God, religion and spirituality. She was never quite sure what she believed and described herself as somewhere between atheism and agnosticism. I, on the other hand, have no such doubts. I shared with her my absolute certainty in God and a benev- olent universe. While somewhat skeptical, she allowed me my new age beliefs and many a lively conversation ensued.

One day she was particularly despondent. When I asked what was wrong, she asked me, "Do you believe in world peace?" I replied without hesitation, "Absolutely, why do you ask?" "My children just don't get along. I am an old woman and I'm so tired of it. They're grown now. Why can't they just get along?" I let her go on. "I'm so tired of the fighting. All they do is fight. I turn on the news and there's more fighting. It will never end. I know you have this belief in God and spirit and all that stuff, but I don't see it." I don't know if she wanted an answer, but I gave her one anyway.

I explained to her that people don't get along because they don't allow others to truly be themselves. We all carry around a mental check-list of how others should be, act and think. When we observe that others do not meet our expectations of acceptable thought and behavior, then conflict becomes inevitable as people seek to move others to conformity. Conflicts in families and relation- ships will end when all persons involved give up their need to be right. Conflicts disappear when people can relinquish their requirement of "right" or "wrong" let themselves consider that perhaps there is no "right" or "wrong," it just is, as it is.

What I am suggesting here goes further

89

than simple tolerance. For true peace to be had, we not only must we be willing to forego our check-list for others, we must also foster an environment where the other has total freedom to be as they are, each holding to the tenet of their own check-list for self and no other. That is Love; allowing the other total freedom and space to be as they are, as they choose to be.

How many of us can really do that? How many of us truly have the capacity to let others be as they are without judgment, requirement or condemnation? Very few of us have this capacity and so we have conflict. We are unable to do it in our homes, in our neighborhoods, in our local communities, in the global community and so we have bitterness, resentment, conflict, and war as each side pushes the other to conform to the prescribed "right," our approved check-list.

Most relationship conflicts would disappear with this one practice: Space must be given to the other to be as they are. Those who have read Conversations with God will always ask themselves, "What would Love do now?" Love is freedom, space, acceptance, fully embracing the other without requirement

And so we debated, Ms. Joyce and I. When all was said, she agreed I had a good theory but couldn't see that it could ever happen, people being who they are. As we continued to dialogue on this topic for weeks and months, she came to the conclusion that maybe the best she could do was to let the situation be as it is, to give up her requirement that they be able to get along. And so she found her peace, not from the requirement that her children be in harmony, but by allowing the situation to be as it is.

As for conflict resolution, I can only speak of my experience and I offer my own life as testimony to the ability to live without conflict. I have no requirements, hold no grudges and therefore live a life rich in humor, joy and serenity. Goodness, abundance and love are all around us and we will see it when we take our eyes off of our check-list of requirements and let it be as it is. When we can get to this point, not only will we enjoy peace in our families and neighborhoods, world peace can truly be had.

So today I reflect on Ms. Joyce and our conversations. Although she often disagreed with my spiritual philosophy, she always allowed me space and love to be me. She gave me total freedom to be Who I Am, without requirement. That is the only love that is real, the only real gift that we can give or receive. The family is still in conflict, worse than when we first spoke of it. The global situation is still in escalation. But I hold fast to my belief: conflict can only exist in our requirement that the other give up Who They Truly Are.

I also hold fast in this: One of the greatest gifts that Ms. Joyce can receive is watching her children put aside their resentments, tear up their check-lists, eliminate their rancor and find true joy in each other, just as she has found in each of them.

And so we wait, Ms. Joyce and I, for Veronica, John Paul, Christina and Ginger to put aside the armor, put down the blame, be done with the complaints and get on with Love. From what I've seen, it's the only thing that works and the only way true happiness can ever be found. And when it happens, all will have received the greatest gift of all—Love.

*"Do your little bit of good where you are;
it's those little bits of good
put together that overwhelm the world."*

ARCHBISHOP DESMOND TUTU

"If my hands are fully occupied
in holding onto something,
I can neither give nor receive."

DOROTHEE SOLLE

The Good Daddy

Mary Mullins

Driving along one day, a fellow motorist mentioned to me that my tire was going flat, so I promptly turned into the nearest gas station. As luck would have it, they did not change tires. (This was many years ago.) It happened that a young father with his two little kids in tow were getting gas. I asked the man if he knew where a station was in the area where I could get my tire changed. He said, "Sorry, no."

I was not worried as I had AAA service. My problem was that I was meeting my friend for lunch. I called AAA and they informed me it would be forty-five minutes to an hour before someone would arrive. I called the restaurant and left a message for my friend and sat in the car to wait.

It was only a few minutes later when the young father pulled up, got out with his kids and said, "We are here to change your tire."

Flabbergasted, I told him how much I appreciated that. When he was finished, I knew he would not accept anything for himself, but I was hoping I might offer something for the children. He gathered his kids around and said, "Oh, no thanks. It was our pleasure." He put the kids in the car and as he passed by me he whispered, "I just wanted to teach them how to be kind."

I whispered back, "You are a good daddy and they are very lucky kids."

93

The Homer Mabry Gambit

Terry Bell

There's a scene in Terms of Endearment where the Debra Winger character, wife of a university teaching assistant with two small children, is in the checkout line at a grocery store and realizes she doesn't have enough money to pay. The cashier begins to berate her when the John Lithgow character steps up and gives Debra Winger the extra money she needs. Debra Winger is embarrassed but accepts the favor. John Lithgow is embarrassed, yet is happy to resolve the awkward situation.

We've all been players in, or witnessed, a scene like this. Even as bystanders we share the embarrassment of the lead actors. But I once knew a man who knew how to play this scene in a way that allowed everybody to keep their dignity and had the added advantage of keeping the line moving.

The first firm I joined as a relatively new lawyer had a very senior partner named Homer Mabry. Homer had been there so long he was beyond retired. Our firm didn't use the term emeritus for its senior lawyers, but if it had, Homer would have qualified. Homer had forgotten more law than most of us would ever learn, and was always happy to share what he knew. It was amazing how often the other end of a telephone conversation with an out-of-town client or attorney would begin with, "Say, how's Homer Mabry?"

It was Homer's practice, when encountering a new attorney in the building cafeteria, to insist on buying his or her lunch. Now, this was at a time when salaries offered beginning lawyers by large firms was starting the exponential increases that continue to this day. So when Homer offered to buy my lunch one day, my first thought was that I well might have already been taking home more than he was. When I protested that it was not necessary for Homer to buy lunch, he said that it was something he liked to do for young lawyers, and that someday I would be in a position to do the same for some other young fellow.

Over time I've reflected on Homer's rejoinder and come to believe that it offers the perfect escape from the inevitably awkward situation that results when you come to the rescue of someone who is liquidity challenged. By characterizing the kindness as a helping hand, to be offered in turn to another, either tomorrow or years from now, the gift is transformed into a loan. And not the kind of loan that requires the "donee" to go through the motions of asking for the kind of personal information that would enable them to put a check in the mail, but that the donor well may not want to give out, but a loan that almost certainly will be repaid on terms suitable to the donor and the donee.

Embarrassing someone in public is never a good idea, of course. Not only does Homer's reassurance free the donee to accept a gift without guilt or embarrassment, it frees the donor to leap in and help without worrying about embarrassing the donee. All that's required, if the donee feels compelled to refuse the offer, is to reassure him or her that the only payback expected is to do the same for someone else someday.

This process, of course, does not apply to friends and family or others whom you see often enough to keep an actual running total. For example, my golf buddies and I buy each other things from the cart girl all the time and keep only a rough sort of accounting, which we expect to somehow even itself out by the time somebody dies.

Does it work in practice? I attended a basketball game in Austin last year. My team was way behind, so when someone expressed a desire for popcorn I was only too happy to jump up and run outside to get it. At the counter I found myself behind an unhappy customer. He wanted the one dollar size, but only larger sizes were left. Seeing in the resulting impasse an opportunity to put Homer's teaching to use, I stepped up and slapped a dollar on the counter, saying to both customer and clerk that all-purpose Texas phrase, "There you go," preparing as I did so to give Homer's speech to a reluctant recipient.

No rehearsal was necessary. The customer accepted my dollar with a "Thanks" and was gone. So I'm still looking for the chance to apply the Homer Mabry Gambit. I think it will work.

> BY CHARACTERIZING THE KINDNESS AS A HELPING HAND, TO BE OFFERED IN TURN TO ANOTHER, EITHER TOMORROW OR YEARS FROM NOW, THE GIFT IS TRANSFORMED INTO A LOAN.

95

The Long Road Home

By Peggy Boice

It was in the early 1990s that I saw the face of God. But I'm getting ahead of myself. Let me start from the beginning. I was living in Austin and had been to Houston to visit my sister and her family. It was a hot Sunday afternoon when I left her house and started home on Interstate 10. An hour out of Houston, I was already in Columbus at the turnoff for Highway 71 that takes you to Austin.

That is when it happened. I suddenly noticed that the "hot" light on my dashboard was lit up. My heart began racing, but I told myself to calm down, move to the shoulder of the road and look for a service station. This was the era before cell phones. Unfortunately, I had no coins or change of any kind in my purse or car, so I couldn't even make a phone call.

I started looking for anyone who could help. As I drove through Columbus, it looked like the town in that movie about the end of the world. There wasn't a single service station open (since it was in the days of "blue laws" that prohibited businesses from being open on Sundays). And, as I said, I didn't have coins for the one pay phone that I saw.

I continued on. Traveling about twenty miles per hour on the shoulder of Highway 71, it took me a full seven hours before I finally came to the outskirts of Austin. As I topped the hill near the old Bergstrom Air

force Base, I could see the lights of Austin across the horizon, and finally breathed, feeling I would make it home safely.

Then it happened. My lights went off and my car went dead. I coasted into what I thought was a full-service gas station. Instead, it was just a Texaco station with a snack shop in it. I stopped my car and walked through the dark parking lot to the shop. I was near tears. I told the lady at the counter that I needed someone to help me jump-start my car.

But she said she couldn't leave her post at the cash register. Tears welled up in my eyes and I started shaking. Standing in front of me and almost out the door was a young woman who looked like she lived around there. She listened and turned back; she said she would be happy to help me with the jumper cables, but she had none. I told her I had some, and felt joy overwhelm me. We went to the car and then realized we had absolutely no idea how to use the cables. I thought I recalled reading that you could blow up your engine if you did it wrong.

So there we stood, helpless. About that time this old rickety car came clanging up to us. It had to be thirty years old. Slowly the driver's window rolled down and a very snagged-toothed old man sat there. He looked tired and worn down from the years. I was even a little frightened by him. But then I looked at his shirt and clear as day it said, "Joe's Car Repair Shop."

So the nice young woman left me in the hands of "Joe" and she drove off. Joe was able to jump-start the car and get it running fairly quickly, but then asked me how far I had to go to get home. I told him it was at least another twenty miles. So he said, "Follow me around back. I have a car repair shop in one of those storage bins."

Skeptical, I hesitated. I was sure it was a ploy to get me out back and do terrible things to me. He saw the fear on my face and said, "Look. You can roll up your windows and lock your doors. I just want to take a look under your car to see what's going on."

I dutifully followed old Joe behind the service station, along a dark path surrounded by storage bins, to one at the end of the row. He got out of his car and opened the garage door to the bin and sure enough, there were all the tools of a car repair shop.

I sat in my car for another hour, as Joe poked and prodded under my car. Finally I heard this loud "thud" as the car shook. Startled from near sleeping, I looked up to see Joe wiping his hands on an old rag. I rolled down the window a crack and asked him what happened. He said, "Well, your transmission was falling out, so I just took a two-by-four board and crammed it up to hold your transmission in."

Dumbfounded, I asked if that was a safe thing to do and if I could still drive the car. He said it would be fine to get me home, but to have my car towed to a repair shop the next day.

It then hit me that I had no way to pay him. All I had was one credit card and absolutely no cash. I asked him if he would take my credit card as payment. He said he was sorry but he didn't take credit cards.

My face flushed and I asked him if I could bring him the money the next day. He replied, "No, it's not necessary little lady. I was just out getting milk for my wife, and I'm glad I was there to give you a hand."

Now remember, he had spent well over an hour helping me, and never called to tell his wife where he was. He then added, "The wife and I don't have any children, but if we did and I had a little girl, I would hope someone would take care of her the same way."

It brings tears to my eye to this very day. I finally drove off and made it home safely. The next day when the car dealership towed my car in, they were dumbfounded at the sight. They said they had never seen a two-by-four stuck up under an engine. They were amazed that the car had not caught fire after being driven over seven hours in the heat with the "hot" light on.

The next weekend I drove back to Joe's place so I could pay him. But there was no sign of his shop or of Joe. I went on a weekday, and the same thing—no sign of Joe. For years I wondered about this, until I finally realized that on that terrible day I had seen the face of God.

The Mile

Sumi Mani

I was the chubby, long haired, pre-teen trying to blend in among my peers and be unnoticed. He was the thirty-something-year-old man who wore his shorts too tight, his hair too long, and his glasses too big. He was my coach, and I was his only volleyball player who had not made the infamous "A Team."

Ah, the A Team. This team consisted of those girls who were able to make their serves over the net. The ones who could consecutively bump the ball into the "football goal" looking target on the gym wall. Most importantly, these were the girls who were able to run a mile in under ten minutes.

Now, to all you marathon runners out there, a mile is probably a walk in the park. However, a mile to be run under ten minutes is a marathon for a twelve-year-old girl with a little extra something around her waistline. This never-ending mile was the only obstacle that stood between me and the elite A Team. Each week, I would look on with envy as another girl squealed and jumped her way into the circle of congratulating girls on the A Team. I would picture myself in her position, except I would not squeal or jump around like some giddy two-year-old, of course! My every thought revolved around the A Team and that blasted mile run.

Before I knew it, the final day of try outs

was upon me. As usual, I dressed up along with the rest of the team and walked out to the gym to start my stretching. Coach came out and asked us to run a few laps around the gym as a warm up. I slowly started trudging along, when Coach called me to his office. Here we go, I thought to myself. By this time, I was the only one who was not on the A Team. Might as well have put a big sign over my head that said "Loser," because that was what this stupid mile had led me to become. I slowly made my way into his office and sat down across from him without looking him in the eyes. No need to see the disappointment and feel even more worthless!

"You are going to be on the A Team," he said.

What? Did my ears deceive me, or did he just say that I made the A Team? I was ecstatic! I couldn't believe it! I was going to be part of the "A" Team, and I didn't even have to worry about that mile. I started playing out my grand entrance into the circle of celebrating girls, of course I would not squeal or jump around, I would be calm and composed, maybe a little cheer, or should I just stand with a big smile on my face and let them come to me? Yea, that sounded even better!

"...okay, let's tackle that mile!"

My ears deceived me. They stopped working after he said I was going to be on the A Team. What they failed to catch was his motivational speech that came before the words, "...okay, let's tackle that mile!"

So my nemesis was still there. There was no escaping it; I had to get that mile done in under ten minutes. Let's get the Loser sign back over my head. I walked with Coach to the track. Before me lay the black, tar-laden circle of hell that was keeping me from my moment of glory.

100 Any bit of confidence left when I placed my feet on the starting line and looked up to find an eternity of asphalt. He blew the whistle and I was off. The first lap was not a problem. Hmmm...maybe I can do this. I started to feel confident again, and even picked up my pace. Bad move. Halfway through the second lap, I felt as if my lungs were not doing what my brain commanded them to do. On my third lap, my legs began to feel as if weights had been tied to them. I kept thinking in my head, I can do this! but the message got lost along the way and didn't make it to my heart. By my fourth, and final, lap I was sucking air. I am sure my face was as red as the shirt I was wearing.

I heard screaming, and then saw a figure running towards me. "Keep going, you're almost there!" By this time, my sides were beginning to hurt, and it felt as if a huge boulder was sitting on top of my chest keeping me from getting oxygen. The figure kept getting closer and closer, until he was right next to me. "I know you can do it!" Coach was there running next to me.

I couldn't go on. It was just too painful. I was losing all my will power, when all of a sudden, I felt a hand close around my hand and pull! Coach was holding my hand and running with me. He pulled me all the way to the finish line. He never let go, not once, and he kept encouraging me every last, painful step of the way.

I see him sometimes at the school where I teach. He still looks the same, the shorts are still too tight, the hair is still too long, and the glasses are still too big. I don't know if he remembers me, but I know that I will never forget him, or what he did for me. I think about that day every time I see him, and it always brings a smile to my face.

I finished the mile. What's even more miraculous than that is the fact that I finished it with one whole minute left to spare.

Coach believed in me and helped me achieve what I thought was the impossible. I finally made the "A Team." Coach made the announcement the next day, and what did I do? I squealed and giggled my way into the circle of congratulating girls.

The Power of a Persistent Smile

Tom Kistner

Many years ago I opened a P. O. Box at our main post office. I have now had that address for more than forty years. When there is more mail than the small box can hold, it is removed and a notice is placed in the box that directs the holder to a service window to receive the mail.

I have made a habit all my life to smile at the people I meet and say hello. I did the same when this young man came to the window and I handed him my notice, smiled and said hello. He took the notice without even acknowledging my presence and retrieved the mail for me. I thanked him and he just closed the window. I was disturbed that he had not said anything but went on my way.

This interaction, or lack thereof, continued periodically for the next twenty years and as we both aged, I continued to smile and say hello and he continued to ignore me.

Then one day he looked up smiled and said hello and went off to get the mail. I now get a smile and hello from him each time I see him at the P.O. no matter where he is.

He is a different person when his face lights up with that smile and my heart leaps each time he does. I am happy that I didn't get angry and stop smiling. He is now older and I know he is ill because he walks with a shuffle. I know that my smile towards him is now filled with love and tenderness when his face beams with a smile. He taught me a lesson of silent persistence and patience.

101

There Is Always Something You Can Do

Leslie Gerber

When I was nine, I used to walk to school down a country road. We lived in the last subdivision in Oklahoma City and a big stretch of farmland was between our little neighborhood and school. Most of the kids in the neighborhood got a ride from their parents, but ours thought it was good for us to walk. On the way, there was a rickety old frame farmhouse that nobody seemed to live in or take care of and I always thought it was vacant.

One day a new girl showed up in class and most everyone was making fun of her because of no particularly good reason except that she was new. I felt pretty sorry for her, and it turned out when we left school for the day, that she was walking down that unpaved road. We walked together past the little farm by the creek and then came to the old rickety house. She said she lived there and invited me in. I had never seen anything like it because we always lived in the last new neighborhood of any city we ever lived in. It was old and dirty and there were no doors between the rooms, just sheets hung in the doorways. The whole house smelled bad.

When I went home to tell my mother about it, I asked if there wasn't something we could do. I didn't have any idea what, I just felt bad for her. Her name was Bernice. A few days later, my mother filled several baskets full of clothes she had collected. She had found out that Bernice had brothers, just like I did, and she got my dad to drive us over to Bernice's house with the clothes.

I have no memory about whether this gift was well-received or not. But I received a very warm present, and that was the sense from my mother that there indeed was something we could do. And there always is!

Time and Patience

Kerri Washburn

My husband and I were newlyweds in March 2006. During the course of a year prior to our marriage, we had become very involved in the church we attend. My husband plays in the praise and worship band and I teach five-year-olds' Sunday school. We have felt very blessed by our church family, friends and God.

In July 2006, Scott and I decided to buy a house that was a little out of our price range but we wanted to keep my two children close to their father and the school they attend. Most importantly, we wanted to stay in the same community where our church is located. The house we purchased was in desperate need of updates. The appliances needed to be replaced along with toilets and tubs. Nothing too major. I won't go into the drama of purchasing a house and what is involved, but I will say that the appraisal did not come back in our favor to get cash out to do the updates. Meanwhile, we were gutting the house ourselves trying to save money while applying for a home improvement loan with a bank. We were trucking along and everything was looking great. We were ripping out the cabinets, walls, etc. ourselves to save money. The loan was a go until the inspector from the bank visited the house and told us that a bank could not loan money on a work in progress.

The bank was calling our demolition a work in progress. We were devastated and stuck! We had no financial way of continuing the job ourselves. We were stuck with a mortgage, utility bills, and a rent house. We couldn't move because the new house we purchased was completely gutted. There wasn't a kitchen or a bathroom. The house wasn't livable.

November 2006, four months from the purchase of our dream home and the beginning of a wonderful life together, we could do nothing but be patient, pray and have trust that somehow it would work out. In the meantime, our finances were going south as we were continually digging a deeper debt hole with two homesteads. One Sunday evening, we met with our Life group from church. Scott usually was unable to attend these casual meetings because his Sunday evenings consisted of being at the church leading the youth praise and worship service, but this night he had a break and

103

was able to join me at our Life group meeting. We enjoyed our time with our friends and continued to keep our heads lifted. We were then asked if we had a prayer request. We hesitated because we didn't want to sound like we were complaining over lack of money or sound selfish. Scott set his pride aside for a moment and explained our ordeal with the house, the bank, the remodeling project, or lack there of. We just asked our Life group to pray for us to have patience that God will provide for us somehow. It felt good to open that up to our friends. As we were walking out of the meeting, a member of our Life group asked how much money we needed to complete the remodeling. We bluntly told him around $15,000 give or take. Not thinking anything of the conversation until the gentleman reached into his back pocket and wrote us a check for $15,000.00!

This gift had way more meaning than the dollar amount. This was an interest free loan, we weren't tied to a bank, which would go against our credit, and it made us become more moderate in our remodeling plans. I truly feel that God made us go through this storm so we could appreciate His timing and His plans for us. This was truly a gift of giving and receiving!

What One Comment Can Do

Linda May

A number of years ago, a very good friend asked me to go to lunch. At the time, she was finishing her last year in law school, had survived a divorce and was dating a man she later married. All in all, she was doing very well, even with the angst associated with the Bar Exam. Interestingly enough, she and her eldest daughter were in law school at the same time, albeit different schools.

As we visited, I told her how proud I was of her. She told me that the reason she asked me to lunch was to invite me to her graduation party. Of course, I told her, I'd come. "Oh," she said, "I don't think you understand. I'm only inviting the people who have made a difference in my life."

Believe it or not, I was speechless, and started to cry. One never knows how one has affected another's life. And to be told this, was an amazing gift.

A couple of addenda: Several years later, I told this story to a group of people in a very intimate setting and, again, became emotional. Later on, someone in the group, a professor at A&M, came up to me and said,

"You know, I've been a teacher for a long time, and I never know what kind of an impression I've left on my students. It's rare that a student ever comes back to tell you. The fact that your friend told you how she felt is very special. Cherish it."

I have.

Subsequently, I told the story at a large luncheon where I was the speaker. Without realizing it, my friend was in the audience. When she came up to me afterwards, she was crying. Until then, she had never fully understood the impact of her words.

This was, and remains, one of the most meaningful gifts I've ever received.

105

Who Said Parrots Can't Comprehend?
A Teacher's Story

Deborah K. Frontiera

August is the hottest month of the year in Houston. It's also the beginning of the school year. Another kindergarten teacher and I stood in the shade of the playground's only tree.

"What's with that kid?" I asked, pointing to a boy wandering alone by the fence, flapping his hands like a baby bird trying to fly.

"I have no idea," she replied. "He can't do anything. Just sits at his place making noises. He bothers the other kids. I don't know what to do with him. I told his mom maybe he wasn't ready for Kindergarten. She got really angry."

It was obvious to me that the child had special needs. In 1991 I had a full week of training on the Least Restrictive Environment and the inclusion of special needs children in regular classrooms. It prepared me for a child with Down syndrome I had volunteered to take into my class.

I had many other children with special needs after that and was the only kindergarten teacher at my school with inclusion training. It was a philosophy I firmly believed in because my husband and one of my daughters are dyslexic. My husband teaches advanced placement Calculus in high school but has difficulty writing a coherent sentence. Our daughter struggled to learn to read, yet earned a bachelor's degree.

Still, I was glad the child on the playground was not "my problem." He represented another side of the inclusion issue. The district I worked for has always been stingy in providing aides for children in inclusion classrooms. I had been lucky that the children placed with me over the years had not truly needed one.

I continued to watch my colleague struggle with the little boy, whose name I learned was Armand. It wore on me. Finally, I asked her, "I'm the one with the inclusion training. Why is he in your class?"

"I have no idea."

Rumors began to float around that Armand's mother, Ruth, was not pleased with his placement and was not pleasant to work with. I say rumors because information about any child's problems or placement is strictly confidential. But any casual observer could see that Armand was different, and parents in any neighborhood talk to each other freely.

My conscience would not let me continue to stand on the sideline. I went to see my principal and suggested that Armand be moved to my class. She looked greatly relieved and thanked me for my offer.

"It will only be for a few weeks until we have an ARD to move him to a self-contained class at another school." An "ARD" is a mandate from the Admission, Review, Dismissal Committee.

Those words were a relief to me. I could live with anything for a few weeks. I decided to try to treat Armand as normally as possible and not worry about academics.

The next morning, Armand's mother brought him to me. She stayed a few minutes while I guided him to a seat on the rug with the other children. I always have children sit in a "u" shape for group lessons. Everyone can see everyone else and me. I put Armand at the end of the "u" on my left. He stared off into space and mumbled nonsense.

"Boys and girls," I said, "this is Armand. He's been having a little trouble with some things, so we will have to help him." The class nodded and smiled. Five-year-olds are generally accepting and require minimal explanation.

Armand's mother and I talked after school. "We don't know what's wrong," she said. "We are trying to get an appointment with a specialist. His little brother isn't like this at all." She confessed that seeing the younger child progress more quickly than Armand had was their first clue that he was not following normal developmental patterns.

"What special education label does he have at this time?" I asked.

"Special education label?"

Her complete bewilderment helped me realize why he'd been "misplaced." I explained my position as the "inclusion" teacher. If the people in the school office did not know about a child's special needs, then class assignment was random. I apologized for the difficulties and said, "Armand should probably have been assigned to me in the first place."

A look of utter relief came over her face, as if everything would be fine now. Inside, I wondered whether I would be up to the challenge and whether I could meet her high expectations.

Every year I seem to have one or two children I refer to as "mother hens." Usually, but not always girls, they can pick up the entire room in five minutes and have everything in the right place. They know the location of the nurse's office by instinct and can be trusted to take a classmate there, or anywhere else in the building. Open and loving, they accept everybody and take care of them. Armand would need someone like that, so I put his laminated name tag at a table right next to one of that year's "mother hens."

She adopted him immediately. If he couldn't do his work, she helped him when hers was finished. If he began to wander away from the playground, she would come running to tell me. "That's okay, Armand, keep trying," was her mantra.

Armand's echolalia drove us all to distraction at times. If a classmate said, in a voice louder than I permitted, "Armand, stop that!" he immediately parroted, "Armand, stop that!"

I would put my hand on the irritated

child's shoulder and say, "If you are absolutely quiet, he won't have anything to copy." That isn't easy for any five-year-old. But it worked—sometimes.

It was even more difficult when he repeated everything I said while teaching. But if I called on him to speak, he lapsed into silence or flapped his hands in frustration. Fortunately, the other children rarely laughed at him. Five-year-olds are incessant talkers until you invite them to speak to the entire group. Perhaps they could all relate to Armand on that level.

The first time Armand stood before the class for "show and tell," he froze. I placed a hand gently on his shoulder and said, "That's okay. Hold up what you brought so the class can see it." His stiff arms lifted the toy slightly, but he said nothing. I invited the children to ask questions. Armand responded by nodding or shaking his head. It was a start.

The "few weeks" until the ARD meeting stretched into a month, then two, as doctor appointments and testing dates went through delay after delay. Under Mother Hen's care, Armand's hand flapping diminished and almost disappeared. The echolalia decreased to a manageable level. In the quiet of nap time, Armand actually read short books to me and began to respond to questions with one word answers.

Ruth found out about a special music program and enrolled Armand in it. He began to learn to play the violin. My little parrot began to stretch his wings and attempt to fly.

It was January before all the testing was finished and the diagnosis in. Armand's mother gave me a copy of the doctor's report and recommendations. Armand had Pervasive Developmental Disorder, a form of Autism.

The doctor also recommended an aide for his classroom.

My administrators still supported placement in the self-contained class at another school. I was afraid another change in Armand's schedule and surroundings would negate all the progress he had made. He would definitely need a smaller group and more intensive one-on-one instruction in first grade, but for now I felt the social skills were more important.

I called Ruth at home the evening before the ARD meeting and told her how I felt. She agreed. "You have to be the one to bring up the need for an aide. I've been told not to mention it. They'll say there is no money in the budget, but you must get the need for an aide into the minutes."

Ethics and protocol and following the law in ARD meetings can be tricky things. I had often bucked "the system" when it came to meeting a child's needs. The system and I didn't get along well. Armand's mother had mentioned the word "lawyer" on more than one occasion. The system didn't like her either. I had taken Armand into my class reluctantly, but now I couldn't see him anywhere else.

My principal was quietly surprised at the turn of events during that long, tense meeting. "We'll check into an aide" was all she said about that issue. I knew it would go no further. We all checked "Agree" on the forms.

In May, Armand stood before the class for "show and tell" with his violin.

"This is my violin," he said in a clear, calm voice. "I am learning how to play it."

I bit back tears of joy and pride.

108